Presented to

_____

From

_____

Date

_____

3 - MINUTE DEVOTIONS
for Christmas

JANICE THOMPSON

BARBOUR BOOKS
An Imprint of Barbour Publishing, Inc.

© 2015 by Barbour Publishing, Inc.

ISBN 978-1-63409-200-5

eBook Editions:
Adobe Digital Edition (.epub) 978-1-63409-593-8
Kindle and MobiPocket Edition (.prc) 978-1-63409-594-5

Published by Barbour Books, an imprint of Barbour Publishing, Inc., P.O. Box 719, Uhrichsville, Ohio 44683, www.barbourbooks.com

Member of the
Evangelical Christian
Publishers Association

Our mission is to publish and distribute inspirational products offering exceptional value and biblical encouragement to the masses.

Printed in the United States of America.

Introduction

*A*h, Christmas! What a blissful time of year. We gather together with loved ones to celebrate the birth of our Savior. We sing carols of joy, unwrap gifts around the tree, and eat until we can't squeeze in another bite!

Yes, most Christmas moments are wonderful, aren't they? But with this season also come loneliness, angst, and pain for many. So, as we celebrate the birth of our Savior, while we're singing hymns of remembrance, may we also take the time to focus on keeping our hearts and minds settled. Healthy.

This little devotional was designed for that very reason—to help you celebrate the true reason for the season and to keep your heart in alignment. As you read these words, may you genuinely draw nearer to Jesus. May you see His coming as the gift it was. . .and is.

Merry Christmas to all, and to all. . .happy reading!

Making Memories

* ◆ * ◆ *

We have happy memories of the godly,
but the name of a wicked person rots away.
PROVERBS 10:7 NLT

There's nothing lovelier than making memories, and it doesn't have to be as complicated as you might think. Looking at Christmas lights together. Baking cookies. Making peanut brittle. Building gingerbread houses. A quiet conversation in front of the fireplace. Gathering together to read the Christmas story. Stringing popcorn to put on the tree. Caroling door-to-door. There are numerous ways to make memories with those you love—children, grandchildren, church friends, and so on. While you're at it, why not scrapbook your adventures? That way you'll never forget the wonderful times you had together. For years to come you can look back on the adventures you created with those you love.

* ◆ * ◆ *

Lord, I love making memories. They're so sweet! Give me fun
and creative ideas, I pray, then help me arrange them in such a
way that others have the time of their lives. May I always look
back on this Christmas season with fondness, Father. Amen.

Favor

• ◆ • ◆ •

But the angel said to her, "Do not be afraid, Mary;
you have found favor with God. You will conceive
and give birth to a son, and you are to call him Jesus."
LUKE 1:30–31 NIV

Can you imagine the thoughts running through Mary's head when she received the news that she was expecting? Can you envision her disbelief? Then, add to all of those things, swallowing the idea that this baby was a sign of God's favor? Surely she struggled to see the correlation. Sometimes we struggle, too. We go through seasons that make no sense and yet we read in the Bible that God showers us with His favor. It's time for us to learn—as Mary did—that God will bring order out of chaos, peace out of frustration, and joy out of pain.

• ◆ • ◆ •

Father, I'll admit that I don't often see how You can redeem
certain situations in my life. When I think of them in comparison
to what Mary went through, however, I'm reminded that
You will, indeed, work all things together for my good. Amen.

Birthed in Love

• ◆ • ◆ •

For God so loved the world that he gave his only
begotten Son, that whosoever believeth in Him
should not perish, but have everlasting life.
JOHN 3:16 KJV

The Savior of the world was birthed in love—God's
love for all of mankind. It's easy to believe that of
the babe in the manger, but did you realize that you were
birthed in love, too? The Bible says that we are born of
the flesh and the Spirit. No matter the circumstances
of your natural birth, there's a second birth—when you
accept Jesus Christ as Savior—and that one is bathed in
heavenly love. So, don't ever say that you're an accident,
or have no value. You're a child of the One True King,
after all, and He never makes mistakes.

• ◆ • ◆ •

Lord, I'm so grateful for Your Son, birthed in love. I'm also grateful
that my spirit was reborn—in love—when I gave my heart to You.
Because of this, I have value! Thank You for new life, Father. Amen.

The Son of God

. ◆ . ◆ .

"He will be great and will be called the Son of the Most High.
The Lord God will give him the throne of his father David,
and he will reign over Jacob's descendants forever; his kingdom
will never end." "How will this be," Mary asked the angel, "since
I am a virgin?" The angel answered, "The Holy Spirit will come
on you, and the power of the Most High will overshadow you.
So the holy one to be born will be called the Son of God."
LUKE 1:32–35 NIV

Jesus Christ, Son of the Most High God. What an amazing thought. . .that God would send His only begotten Son into the world. . .for us. That babe in the manger wasn't just Mary's baby boy; He was God's baby boy, too. We can hardly wrap our minds around such a concept, but it's true! One minute in heaven, the next on earth. One minute, seated on a throne and the next, wrapped in swaddling clothes. A whimpering infant, in need of a mother's care, once—and still—the King of all kings. How can we ever thank Him for such a sacrifice. . . and all for us?

. ◆ . ◆ .

Lord, You sent Your Son. Your one and only Son. We are in awe
of such a gift. How did Jesus leave the splendor of heaven?
Surely love for us propelled Him, and we are so grateful! Amen.

Salvation

• ◆ • ◆ •

*"Salvation is found in no one else, for there is no other name
under heaven given to mankind by which we must be saved."*

ACTS 4:12 NIV

There is only one Name under heaven that's powerful enough to save us, and that name is Jesus. The babe in the manger wasn't just a weak infant; He was the King of kings and Lord of lords, the very Savior of the world. When Jesus chose to give His life on the cross, He offered salvation to anyone who would call on His name and accept His gift. So, this Christmas, don't just look at the baby in the manger as the gift. . .examine what He did on the cross, and then unwrap that present. It will save you for all eternity.

• ◆ • ◆ •

*Father, if You hadn't sent Your Son, we would never
have experienced freedom from the curse of sin.
How can we ever thank You? What a gracious God
You are! I'm so grateful for my salvation. Amen.*

Joy

*When Elizabeth heard Mary's greeting, the baby leaped in her
womb, and Elizabeth was filled with the Holy Spirit. In a loud
voice she exclaimed: "Blessed are you among women, and blessed is
the child you will bear! But why am I so favored, that the mother of
my Lord should come to me? As soon as the sound of your greeting
reached my ears, the baby in my womb leaped for joy. Blessed is she
who has believed that the Lord would fulfill his promises to her!"*

LUKE 1:41–45 NIV

Coming into God's presence is a joyful experience!
We don't have to approach His throne with fear and
trembling, wondering if He'll chide us for all we've done
wrong. We can come boldly, knowing He reaches out to
us with open arms, ready to share our burdens, lift our
spirits, and give us wisdom to face life's challenges. Best
of all, we can experience joy because we know that the
Lord wants to forgive our sins. So, boldly approach His
throne, then, as with Elizabeth, be ready for a joy-burst
in your spirit!

*Lord, I've experienced such joy in Your presence. Thank You for
welcoming me. I don't have to be afraid when I'm with You. Amen.*

Giving

*But this I say, He which soweth sparingly shall reap also sparingly;
and he which soweth bountifully shall reap also bountifully.*
2 CORINTHIANS 9:6 KJV

Even the Scrooges of this world get the gift-giving
bug at Christmastime. Most, anyway. There's just
something about this joyous season that makes us feel like
giving to one another. But, why? Did you ever think about
the logic behind gifts? Why do we feel so compelled to
give things away, often things that will break or be out of
fashion in just a few years? Does this make any sense at
all? And yet, we shop until we drop, wrap with the best
ribbons and bows, and lovingly present our gifts to those
we love, hopeful they will receive them with great joy and
admiration. The look of delight on the faces of those we
love makes all of the shopping worth it, all of the hours
wrapping gifts less stressful.

* ◆ * ◆ *

*Lord, I want to be known as a giver, not a taker.
Reestablish that idea in my heart this Christmas. May I
reflect Your heart for others with every single gift! Amen.*

Stress

• ◆ • ◆ •

"Peace I leave with you; my peace I give you.
I do not give to you as the world gives. Do not
let your hearts be troubled and do not be afraid."
JOHN 14:27 NIV

Christmas was never meant to be a stressful season. All of the crazy-dash-about-materialistic-gotta-spend-more-than-I-make stuff was never God's idea in the first place. He meant for Christmas to be a peaceful, calm season of reflection and thanks for the gift of the baby in the manger. This year, instead of giving in to the temptation to rush, rush, rush, and buy, buy, buy, why not pause and reflect, instead? Find peaceful ways to celebrate. Your stress will lift as you shift your focus from "what I have to do" to "what God did for me."

• ◆ • ◆ •

Father, I'm grateful for the reminder that You never
meant for Christmas to be chaotic. With You it was
always about relationship not about outdoing one another.
Thanks for that reminder, Lord. Amen.

Food

• ◆ • ◆ •

Always be joyful. Pray continually, and give thanks whatever
happens. That is what God wants for you in Christ Jesus.
1 Thessalonians 5:16–18 ncv

*W*hen you think of Christmas, likely you think of
food, especially desserts! Yummy pies. Cookies,
decorated by the children in your life. Glazed ham with
all of the trimmings. Christmas is definitely a time to fill
up on the good stuff! This year, as you're going through
your recipe box, don't forget to add one very special
ingredient: joy. Sometimes, in the hustle and bustle of
food prep, you can get a little overwhelmed. Exhausted,
even. As you're preparing foods this season, think of
the blessing that chocolate pie will be to Aunt Mary.
Contemplate the reaction from Grandma Rosey as she
sees the sweet potato casserole. Focus on those you're
preparing for, not just the food itself. Have a giver's
mindset and the whole experience will be a piece of cake.
(Get it? Piece of cake?)

• ◆ • ◆ •

Thank You, Lord, for the reminder that even my food
preparation time can be joyous! Remind me of those I'm
cooking for as I'm working, then give me joy as I work. Amen.

A Sign

"Therefore the Lord himself will give you a sign: The virgin will conceive and give birth to a son, and will call him Immanuel."
ISAIAH 7:14 NIV

How many times do we use the words, "Lord, if You want me to do this, please show me some kind of sign." Sometimes He does, and we move forward. Sometimes the supposed lack of a sign causes us to stop in our tracks. Long before God sent His Son into the world, He promised a particular "sign," something that the people could be watching for: A virgin would be with child. Never before in the history of mankind and never since has a virgin ever given birth. That one fact, by itself, still stands at the top, "sign of all signs." But wait, there's more! The child born of this virgin would be a boy. How, thousands of years ago, could the sex of a child be told before birth? There were no ultrasounds, after all. And this babe's name? Even that was prophesied! *Emmanuel*, which means "God with us."

* ◆ * ◆ *

Lord, I can't imagine what the people of Isaiah's time must've been thinking when this Word came forth! What faith it must have taken to believe for three separate miracles in one: a virgin birth. The sex of the child. And, ultimately, the idea that God Himself, would be joining them on earth. Remarkable! Amen.

Togetherness

• ◆ • ◆ •

I in them and You in me—so that they may be brought
to complete unity. Then the world will know that You
sent me and have loved them even as You have loved me.
JOHN 17:23 NIV

Togetherness. We all know what it means: people coming together. But just "being" together isn't really what togetherness is all about. You can be in a room filled with people and still be out of unity, after all. When we come together during the Christmas season (and other times of the year), God longs for us to be in unity—to operate as one. Sure, we're all individuals, but we're one big happy family in Him. So put those squabbles and "must be right" attitudes aside. This year it's all about togetherness.

• ◆ • ◆ •

Lord, I love it when those I love are gathered close.
This Christmas season I pray for complete unity. May we all be
in one accord as we gather to celebrate Your Son's birth. Amen.

Salvation

• ◆ • ◆ •

"She will give birth to a son, and you are to give him the name Jesus,
because he will save his people from their sins."
MATTHEW 1:21 NIV

What a mesmerizing concept: a baby who had the power to save people from sin. Can you imagine what Mary must've thought when she received word that the child inside of her had that kind of power? Surely she doubted; if even for a moment. No human being in the history of the world could save people from sin. Only God could do that. As Mary wrapped her brain around that idea, perhaps she came to grips with the "God Incarnate" truth: The Lord, Himself, had truly come to dwell with (and in her case, inside) mankind. And all for one reason: to bring salvation.

• ◆ • ◆ •

Father, what a gift! Salvation. Only You can save me from
my sins—the ones I committed yesterday and the ones I've yet to
commit. How can I ever thank You for sending Jesus to
wash away my sins? I'm eternally grateful. Amen.

Born of the Spirit

• ◆ • ◆ •

This is how the birth of Jesus the Messiah came about: His mother
Mary was pledged to be married to Joseph, but before they came
together, she was found to be pregnant through the Holy Spirit.
MATTHEW 1:18 NIV

Think about these words: "found to be with child." In
the days of Mary and Joseph, those very words could
have been a death sentence for Mary. To be with child
out of wedlock was unthinkable. And yet. . .God chose to
move in this way, against the norms of society and reason,
to bring His Son into the world. Mary's parents and other
members of the community were surely doubtful when
she explained the logistics of the pregnancy, but God
proved Himself time and time again—through angels,
shepherds, and even wise men. This special babe was,
indeed, out of this world, born of the very Spirit of God.
And we, too, can be born of the Spirit, thanks to His
sacrifice.

• ◆ • ◆ •

God, You are Father, indeed! Father of all mankind and Father to
Your own Son, conceived by Your Spirit. Thank You that I can be
born of the Spirit, too. What an eternal blessing! Amen.

Holy Government

• ◆ • ◆ •

For to us a child is born, to us a son is given,
and the government will be on his shoulders.
ISAIAH 9:6 NIV

How wonderful, to live in a country (or city or state) that honors God! When government leaders acknowledge the King of kings and Lord of lords as ruler over all, the people live in peace. But when our leaders turn away from God, the consequences are far-reaching. When Jesus came as a babe in the manger, He established a different sort of government: one that starts in the heart. When men and women wrap their minds around this concept—that good government begins in the heart—it will change cities, states, nations. . .and even the world!

• ◆ • ◆ •

Lord, begin in me! May my heart be governed by Your Spirit.
I want to be a city changer, a state changer, and a world changer!
Rule and reign in my heart, I pray. Amen.

The Holy Child's Names

• ◆ • ◆ •

And he will be called Wonderful Counselor,
Mighty God, Everlasting Father, Prince of Peace.
ISAIAH 9:6 NIV

Naming a child is so much fun. We choose from our family tree, or pick brand-new-to-us names. Some even pick unusual names with unique spellings, just to be different. Before Mary even spoke the name "Jesus" the baby had already been given a host of names: Wonderful Counselor. Mighty God. Everlasting Father. Prince of Peace. Wow! Not your usual Tom, Dick, or Harry! Isaiah prophesied this babe's name—actually, names—over a thousand years before His birth. Talk about an anticipated child! And no one will ever forget the most precious name of all: Jesus.

• ◆ • ◆ •

Lord, how amazing it must have been, to hear the names of Your Son
spoken by Your creation for the first time. When Isaiah breathed the
words: Wonderful Counselor, Mighty God, Everlasting Father,
Prince of Peace. . .how Your heart must've leapt! And mine is leaping
now, at the very mention of His Name. Praise You, Lord! Amen.

Jesus Will Reign

• ◆ • ◆ •

Of the greatness of his government and peace there will be no end.
He will reign on David's throne and over his kingdom, establishing
and upholding it with justice and righteousness from that time on
and forever. The zeal of the LORD Almighty will accomplish this.
ISAIAH 9:7 NIV

Sometimes we go through hard seasons and wonder if God is still on the throne. It feels like He's gone missing. The truth is that His reign will never end. In good times and bad—from now until eternity—He's there. When we're struggling to pay the bills or purchase gifts for the grandkids at Christmas, He reigns. When we're celebrating the birth of a child, He reigns. When we're facing the loss of a loved one, He's still right there, on the throne. He doesn't take a tumble whenever we go through a rough situation. The key to knowing true peace is to keep the Prince of Peace in His rightful place—enthroned on our hearts.

• ◆ • ◆ •

Lord, You reign! I don't always acknowledge that, but You do.
May You reign in my heart today. May You reign in my thoughts
and my actions. I praise You because You are worthy. Amen.

Divine Appointment

• ◆ • ◆ •

In those days Caesar Augustus issued a decree that a census should be taken of the entire Roman world. (This was the first census that took place while Quirinius was governor of Syria.) And everyone went to their own town to register. So Joseph also went up from the town of Nazareth in Galilee to Judea, to Bethlehem the town of David, because he belonged to the house and line of David.
LUKE 2:1–4 NIV

Mary and Joseph ended up in Bethlehem not by choice, but by divine appointment. Because Joseph was "of the house and lineage of David" he had to go to Bethlehem to register for the census. Oh, but God had something much bigger in mind! It was prophesied hundreds of years prior that out of tiny Bethlehem—an inconsequential place—would come One who would rule Israel. And rule, He did! During this special season, look for divine appointments. See your comings and goings through God's eyes. Who will you meet along the way? Who can you minister to? Who can you pray for? These special appointments are strategically coordinated by God, not just during the Christmas season, but year-round.

• ◆ • ◆ •

Lord, thank You for the reminder that You have divine appointments waiting for me. Like Mary and Joseph I want to be in the right place at the right time. Guide my steps, Father, I pray. Amen.

Awkward Travels

• ◆ • ◆ •

*He went there to register with Mary, who was pledged
to be married to him and was expecting a child.*
LUKE 2:5 NIV

Can you picture Mary and Joseph traveling by donkey
to Bethlehem. . .Mary, huge with child, and Joseph,
fretting all the way? What a trip that must've been.
They made it safely to their destination and we know
the rest of the story—the Christ Child was born in a
stable, Savior of the world, come to dwell among men in
the lowliest of conditions. Perhaps your holiday season
involves "awkward travel," too. Maybe you have to cross
the country across snowy, icy roads to spend time with
loved ones. Or maybe you're heading back to a place
that stirs up uncomfortable memories. Regardless, just
remember that God saw Mary and Joseph through the
toughest journey of all and He will go with you, too.
If you submit your plans to Him, the outcome will be
glorious!

• ◆ • ◆ •

*Father, I submit my travel plans to You. Lead, guide, and protect,
I pray. May my journeys be memorable and safe, Lord. Amen.*

No Room in the Inn

• ◆ • ◆ •

So it was, that while they were there, the days were completed
for her to be delivered. And she brought forth her firstborn Son,
and wrapped Him in swaddling cloths, and laid Him in a
manger, because there was no room for them in the inn.
LUKE 2:6–7 NKJV

How scared Mary must have been when she heard
the words, "There's no room in the inn." No place
to rest her head? No safe place to deliver the baby? No
doubt fear came upon her! Maybe you know what it
means to hear the "no room" speech, too. You try to fit
into a certain crowd and they nudge you out. You long to
find a place of comfort and peace, but it seems to elude
you. Here's good news this Christmas season! God had a
better plan for Mary and Joseph. He knew the inn would
be full and had already made provision elsewhere. He's
done the same for you. No matter what you're hoping
for, He's already made provision. Whether it's relational,
emotional, or otherwise, God has gone ahead of you and
set His plans in motion. So don't fret! The door of the
inn might be closed, but there's better lodging ahead.

• ◆ • ◆ •

Lord, I trust Your plans for my life. I might not always get
what I want, but You have better things in mind for me than
I could dream for myself. Thank You for that, Father! Amen.

Angels from On High

• • ◆ •

Now there were in the same country shepherds living out in the
fields, keeping watch over their flock by night. And behold,
an angel of the Lord stood before them, and the glory of the
Lord shone around them, and they were greatly afraid.
LUKE 2:8–9 NKJV

Perhaps you know someone personally who claims to
have seen an angel. The Bible says they're all around
us, after all—protecting, even warring on our behalf.
And they were there on the night the Christ Child was
born, too. Lowly shepherds kept watch over their flocks
by night. . .as always. They did their usual thing in the
usual way. Then, the most unusual thing happened! The
glory of the Lord shone around them. It lit up the sky
in heavenly display and the angel of the Lord appeared
on the scene, followed by a host of others. Wow! Picture
yourself in that place. What would you have done?

• ◆ • ◆ •

Lord, I'm not sure what I would have done, if I'd been in
the field that night. Chances are pretty good I would've
screamed and then run for the hills! Thank You for Your
presence on that holy night. I'm so grateful the shepherds
listened and followed the instructions they were given.
May I do the same, each time You speak to my heart. Amen.

Great News

• ◆ • ◆ •

But the angel reassured them. "Don't be afraid!" he said.
"I bring you good news that will bring great joy to all people.
The Savior—yes, the Messiah, the Lord—has been
born today in Bethlehem, the city of David!"
LUKE 2:10–11 NLT

There are so many "big news days." All you have to do is turn on the television to see startling (and sometimes horrific) news stories. We cluster around our televisions, wanting every detail. Of course we are drawn to the news for other reasons, too. During a political season we want to see which candidate will come out on top. During inclement weather we watch to see if—or when—it will be safe to travel. Yes, the news is readily available these days. But think about how news spread two thousand years ago—before the Internet, before television, radio, or any other forms of mass communication. People heard the news—good and bad—as it traveled from person to person, by word of mouth. And yet, the story of Christ's birth was told, and told, and told again!

• ◆ • ◆ •

I love good news, Lord! Thank You for the reminder that
Christmas brings the very best news of all: the story of a God
who loves us so much that He sent His only begotten Son. Amen.

Looking for a Sign

• ◆ • ◆ •

And this shall be a sign unto you; Ye shall find the
babe wrapped in swaddling clothes, lying in a manger.
LUKE 2:12 KJV

Can you imagine the poor shepherds, searching throughout Bethlehem to find the Christ Child? How many doors would they have to knock on until they got the right one? Fortunately, they didn't have to knock on even one! They were given holy guidance from the get-go: "You will find a baby wrapped in cloths and lying in a manger." A manger? Must've seemed a strange place. Sometimes God gives us signs, too. He whispers, "Don't go there!" or "Send your friend a note today" messages. If we're really tuned in, these signs (God-directions) can be life changing. Like the shepherds, we're on an amazing mission every day of our lives. We're not headed to Bethlehem to search for the babe in the manger, but we are headed into our circle of influence to change lives.

• ◆ • ◆ •

I'm grateful for the signs You've placed all around me, Lord.
May my eyes always be open to Your guidance, I pray. Amen.

Peace on Earth

• ◆ • ◆ •

And suddenly there was with the angel a multitude of
the heavenly host praising God, and saying, Glory to God
in the highest, and on earth peace, good will toward men.
LUKE 2:13–14 KJV

Peace on earth." Such a simple phrase, one that we
always hear at Christmastime. And yet, what a
complicated process. All it takes is one glance at the news
to know that our world is anything but peaceful. Hatred
doesn't take a sabbatical, even during the Christmas
season. That's why we have to continue to ask God to
grant peace on earth, not just during the holidays, but all
year long. Only He can calm the anger in an evildoer's
heart and prevent a terrorist act before it happens. Only
He can minister to the turmoil in a single mother's heart
or the pain in a widow's lonely hours. God is the giver
of peace and we must continue to call on Him to bring
peace—true, lasting peace—on earth.

• ◆ • ◆ •

Father, so many people are hurting and the holidays only
seem to exaggerate that for some. Please calm the hearts of
those who are angry, bring comfort to those who are hurting,
and peace to those who are in turmoil. Amen.

Walking in Obedience

· ◆ · ◆ ·

When the angels had left them and gone into heaven, the shepherds
said to one another, "Let's go to Bethlehem and see this thing that
has happened, which the Lord has told us about."
LUKE 2:15 NIV

When the shepherds received their instruction from
the angels, they had a choice. They could've stayed
in the field, tending their sheep. In fact, leaving the sheep
alone went against everything inside of them. And yet. . .
they had their marching orders. And so, march they did,
straight to Bethlehem, to the stable, where they found
the young child with His mother. What if the shepherds
had opted to disobey? The entire Christmas story
would've changed. Oh, but they didn't! They listened,
they responded in obedience, and the rest, as they say,
is history! We have a lot to learn from these obedient
shepherds, not just at Christmastime, but year-round.
God gives us marching orders. Will we leave our comfort
zone and travel as the Spirit leads, or will we remain
behind? The choice is up to us.

· ◆ · ◆ ·

Lord, I want to be obedient to Your nudges.
Thank You for giving me more than one chance to obey, Father!
I want to get it right, all year-round! Amen.

Spreading the Word

• ◆ • ◆ •

When they had seen him, they spread the word
concerning what had been told them about this child.
LUKE 2:17 NIV

Do you ever wonder what would have happened if the shepherds hadn't spread the word about baby Jesus' birth? They had a life-changing encounter with the King of kings, dressed in swaddling clothes, no less, and couldn't wait to tell others. God expects the same of us. When we have a life-changing encounter with the Lord, we should be so filled with joy, so overcome with gratitude for His salvation, that we rush to tell others. And, like those who heard the shepherds' story, our friends and loved ones will be just as amazed. How can they not be, when they see the difference our personal encounter with the Lord has made?

• ◆ • ◆ •

Lord, thank You for interrupting my life so that I could
encounter You! Getting to know You has been the best
adventure in my life. Help me spread the word, Father,
so that others can celebrate Your goodness, too. Amen.

Pondering, not Pontificating

• ◆ • ◆ •

*But Mary treasured up all these things
and pondered them in her heart.*
LUKE 2:19 NIV

Have you ever examined Mary's reaction to the news that she would bear the Savior of the world? Perhaps the most compelling part of her story is the fact that she was able to "treasure up" the news and ponder it in her heart. Pondering, not pontificating. Pondering, not questioning. What a wonderful example she set for the rest of us. More often than not, we get shocking news and want to hit the airwaves—telling our friends by phone, text, email, or social media. We don't often pause to simply ponder the news in our hearts. The next time you're faced with troubling news (or life-changing news), stop. Take a moment. Spend some time with God, instead.

• ◆ • ◆ •

Lord, I acknowledge that You're not always the first one I run to when I'm troubled. Unlike Mary, I can't seem to "keep things and ponder them in my heart." Please help me with this, I pray. Amen.

A Reason to Praise

• ◆ • ◆ •

The shepherds returned, glorifying and praising God for all the things they had heard and seen, which were just as they had been told.
LUKE 2:20 NIV

Imagine seeing the King of kings in person. Wow! Talk about a reason to celebrate. Of course the shepherds had no idea what Jesus' life and ministry would look like. They only knew that the Lord had led them to this very special place to see, face-to-face, the One who would change the world. We don't always see the miracles ahead of time either, but there's no reason why we shouldn't go ahead and praise today. God has led us, by His Spirit, to His Son. In the presence of the Savior, we have the hope and assurance that anything we're facing can and will be better. So, what's keeping you? Go ahead and start praising Him today.

• ◆ • ◆ •

Sometimes I feel like those shepherds, Lord. I come into Your presence at Your bidding and hope fills my being. I can't help but praise, even in advance of the miracles You've yet to perform. You give me a reason to praise, Father. Amen.

A Watchful Eye

• ◆ • ◆ •

*After Jesus was born in Bethlehem in Judea, during the time
of King Herod, Magi from the east came to Jerusalem and
asked, "Where is the one who has been born king of the Jews?
We saw his star when it rose and have come to worship him."*
MATTHEW 2:1–2 NIV

The magi (wise men) were keeping a close eye on
the sky. Why? Because they knew, in their spirits
and from careful study of scriptures, that the Messiah
would be coming soon. They set their focus on what
they believed would happen, not what was right in front
of them. We need to learn to do the same. When we're
facing trials we need to shift our gaze to the promise
of what's to come. If we keep a watchful eye on the
promise, we'll maintain hope. If we shift our gaze to the
problem, we'll crater. The wise men were diligent and we
can be, too. And look at the payoff! Because they were
tuned in to God's holy plan, they got to see a miracle
before their very eyes. God wants no less for us. May we
fix our gaze on Him, the giver of hope.

• ◆ • ◆ •

*Lord, I don't want to be distracted. I want to keep my focus on
You. May I remain diligent, Father, with my eyes to the skies,
waiting for You to come through in a marvelous way,
just as You did for those wise men, so many years ago. Amen.*

Bethlehem, a Set-Aside Place

• ◆ • ◆ •

*When King Herod heard this he was disturbed, and all
Jerusalem with him. When he had called together all the people's
chief priests and teachers of the law, he asked them where the
Messiah was to be born. "In Bethlehem in Judea," they replied,
"for this is what the prophet has written."*
MATTHEW 2:3–5 NIV

Bethlehem was the appointed place for the Messiah
to make His entrance in the world. All eyes were
on this tiny place (at least the eyes of those who pored
over the scriptures and believed them to be true). Like
Bethlehem, our hearts are the "appointed place" for the
Messiah, Jesus Christ, to come and dwell. He wants
that set-aside place for Himself, a place where He can
be worshipped and adored. Today, as you think about
Bethlehem, as you ponder the scriptures about the Christ
Child's birth, think of your own heart as a "stable" (a
dwelling place) for the infant King. May He have full
reign in that set-apart place.

• ◆ • ◆ •

*Father, I give You my heart. May You come and dwell there,
just as Your Son dwelt in the manger. Take up residence,
I pray. My heart is wide open, Lord. Enter in. Amen.*

The Least Becomes the Greatest

• ◆ • ◆ •

"But you, Bethlehem, in the land of Judah, are by no means
least among the rulers of Judah; for out of you will come
a ruler who will be the shepherd of my people Israel."
MATTHEW 2:6 NIV

Bethlehem isn't a very big town. To some, it would
appear to be an inconsequential place. Certainly
no comparison to nearby Jerusalem. And yet, the Lord
ordained that, out of this humble place, would come the
Savior, the One destined to change the world. Wow!
God can use the smallest, most seemingly insignificant
thing to astound the world. The same is true today.
He longs to use even the most ordinary person—the
one who feels as if she has little to offer. He can take a
seemingly small, insignificant human being and use her
to affect the lives of those around her. Wow! Talk about
a fantastic, heavenly plan. So don't try to measure your
worth by the world's standards. Just watch and see how
the Lord can—and will—use you for His glory.

• ◆ • ◆ •

Father, like tiny Bethlehem, I sometimes feel insignificant.
Overlooked. But You, oh Lord, have great plans for me!
I give my heart to You and submit myself to Your greater plan.
I can't wait to see what's in store! Amen.

Open Eyes and Hearts

· ◆ · ◆ ·

*Then Herod secretly called the magi and determined from them the
exact time the star appeared. And he sent them to Bethlehem and
said, "Go and search carefully for the Child; and when you have
found Him, report to me, so that I too may come and worship Him."*
MATTHEW 2:7–8 NASB

The magi weren't just tuned in to the stars (open
eyes); they were also tuned in to the motives behind
Herod's request (open hearts). Together they decided
not to return to him or to give him details about where
the Christ Child lay. Why? Because, in keeping their
hearts open to the Lord's leading, they discovered the
truth: Herod wanted to kill the young babe because he
felt threatened by Him. God is still in the business of
leading and guiding those whose hearts are open. He can
give instruction, guidance, warning, and even nudges to
minister to hurting people. Like the magi, we can have
God's eyes and ears, so that we can be more effective in
reaching people for Him.

· ◆ · ◆ ·

*Lord, thank You for the reminder that I need to keep both
my eyes and my heart open. I want to minister to others,
Father, so keep me dialed in to Your master plan. Amen.*

Seeing is Believing

• ◆ • ◆ •

After hearing the king, they went their way; and the star,
which they had seen in the east, went on before them until
it came and stood over the place where the Child was.
When they saw the star, they rejoiced exceedingly with great joy.

MATTHEW 2:9–10 NASB

Have you ever said the words, "I'll believe it when I see it!"? It's just human nature, isn't it? We want to see the proof with our own eyes. In the case of the wise men, they saw, up close and personal, the Savior of the world. Surely, in spite of their psychological preparation, they were overwhelmed. When enough time had passed for the news to sink in, they went on their way, rejoicing and praising God. That's how it is with us, too! When we're convinced in our heart of hearts. . .when we really truly believe we've witnessed something extraordinary. . . we can't help but praise. But here's the key: We can start praising even before we see the miracle! In fact, it brings great joy to God's heart when we praise Him in advance. So what's keeping you? Lift your voice in a song of praise. Maybe, just maybe, you're about to witness a miracle!

• ◆ • ◆ •

Lord, I don't want to wait until I see Your miracles up close and
personal. I want to start praising now. Today I choose to do that, even if
my circumstances aren't what I'd hoped. Praise You, Father! Amen.

Bowing down to Worship

• ◆ • ◆ •

*After coming into the house they saw the Child with Mary His
mother; and they fell to the ground and worshiped Him.*
MATTHEW 2:11 NASB

Have you ever pondered the phrase "bowing down
to worship"? When we come in bowed posture
to worship the King of kings and Lord of lords, we're
humbled. We're submitted. We're not distracted, looking
to the right or the left. We've deliberately closed
ourselves off from the things that want to steal our
attention and we're able to focus solely on Him. Like
the wise men, we can bow the knee, overwhelmed by the
majesty of the King of kings and Lord of lords. There is
no greater posture for the believer than this.

• ◆ • ◆ •

*Father, I come to You today with bowed knee and submitted heart,
ready to worship. I give myself to You, afresh. Like the wise men,
I rid myself of all distractions so that we can spend time together.
How I love You, Lord! Amen.*

Giving God Your Gifts

• ◆ • ◆ •

Then, opening their treasures, they presented
to Him gifts of gold, frankincense, and myrrh.
MATTHEW 2:11 NASB

What a gorgeous presentation those wonderful gifts must have made: gold (an acknowledgement of the baby's kingship), incense (a symbol of the child's deity), and myrrh (used for embalming; a symbol of the child's one-day sacrifice). Mary and Joseph couldn't have understood the implication of each gift at first, but they could certainly see the value. These strangers had just given them real treasures, and, in doing so, had affirmed everything the couple had been told by the angels. When we give gifts, we offer affirmation, too! We tell the recipient, "You're worth the cost. . .and much, much more."

• ◆ • ◆ •

Lord, I get it! The gifts from the wise men weren't
just random offerings; they were carefully thought out.
So, too, can my gifts be to others. Help me as I choose,
that each offering will be tailored to show Your love. Amen.

Listening to God's Voice

• ◆ • ◆ •

Then God spoke to them in a dream. He told them not to go back to Herod. So they went to their own country by another road.
MATTHEW 2:12 NLV

Have you ever wondered what prompted the magi to return home after seeing the baby Jesus? Initially they had planned to return to Herod, to report what they had seen. Then, after "having been warned in a dream," they decided to take a different route, back to their own country, as far from Herod as they could be.

God has all sorts of ways that He speaks to us. He whispers to our hearts. He speaks through His Word. And sometimes He even speaks in a dream. Perhaps you're like the magi. You've made plans to do something and then a "prompting" (a spiritual nudge) sent you off in a different direction. Thank goodness you listened to the prompting! Those little nudges can spare us heartache, pain, and even disaster. God is always speaking, just as He did to the wise men. The real question is, "Are we listening?"

• ◆ • ◆ •

I'm listening, Lord! I really am. Give me direction and then give me the courage to step out in faith as You lead. I want to hear. . .and obey, Father. Amen.

An Unlikely King

• ◆ • ◆ •

Rejoice greatly, Daughter Zion! Shout, Daughter Jerusalem!
See, your king comes to you, righteous and victorious,
lowly and riding on a donkey, on a colt, the foal of a donkey.
ZECHARIAH 9:9 NIV

All of Israel sat waiting, perched, ready for a king, a Savior. They were looking for the usual signs: a crown, a throne. Instead, they got a baby in a manger: hardly what they were seeking, and difficult to wrap their minds around. And that babe in the manger continued to fly in the face of their ideals as He grew. A lowly carpenter. A homeless evangelist. An unusual king, riding on a lowly donkey into Jerusalem just a few days before His crucifixion. Yes, Jesus certainly defied the odds. And yet, He accomplished all the Father sent Him here to accomplish. What about you? Have you defied the odds? Are you accomplishing the tasks set before you? You are a child of the King, after all!

• ◆ • ◆ •

Father, I'm so grateful for the example set by Your Son. He did defy
the odds, Lord, and I can, too! I can be more than others say I can be.
I can do more than even I think I can do. With You on my side,
this next year can be amazing! Thank You for that reminder. Amen.

Peace

• ◆ • ◆ •

"Blessed is the king who comes in the name of the Lord!
Peace in heaven and glory in the highest!"
LUKE 19:38 NIV

There's something so calming about the words, "Sleep in heavenly peace." The word *peace* calms us at once. And the lullaby quality of the song drives home the point that the very atmosphere surrounding the Savior of the world, from His birth in the stable on, was one of intrinsic peace and serenity. When nighttime falls (in a spiritual sense), we can still experience peace. When the "Herods" of this world (those who would oppose us) come looking for us, we can experience peace. When doubters wonder about our story, peace lives on. It's the driving force behind our faith: peace on earth, peace in our hearts, peace in our families, peace in the middle of the storm. This Christmas, as you face the usual (and possibly not-so-usual) issues, think about that baby in the manger. He truly could "sleep in heavenly peace"...and so can you.

• ◆ • ◆ •

Peace, Lord. Thank You for the gift of peace.
When all is whirling around me, I cling to this promise. Amen.

Hope

• ◆ • ◆ •

*May the God of hope fill you with all joy and peace
as you trust in him, so that you may overflow
with hope by the power of the Holy Spirit.*
Romans 15:13 niv

So many times we hear stories about people being
robbed at Christmastime. Their presents are taken,
sometimes from the back of the car while they shop.
Or worse, their homes are invaded and possessions
stolen. We would be devastated to have this happen to
us. Thievery hits at the heart, and not just during the
holidays. Why, then, do we tolerate having our hope
stolen? So many times we allow the enemy of our soul
to rob us of hope, especially at Christmastime. We begin
to replay the video in our head of family problems,
relationship issues, financial woes, and so on. God wants
to restore our hope, not just during the holidays, but
year-round. So cling to His promise of hope. Don't let
anyone—or anything—steal it from you.

• ◆ • ◆ •

*I remain hopeful in You, Lord! I refuse to let anything
rob me of the hope You've placed in my heart. Amen.*

Family

• ◆ • ◆ •

At that time Mary got ready and hurried to a town
in the hill country of Judea, where she entered
Zechariah's home and greeted Elizabeth.
LUKE 1:39–40 NIV

Who did Mary turn to when troubled? Who did she count on to see her through a season of change? Family. She went to her cousin, Elizabeth, for comfort and counsel. And Elizabeth turned out to be just the person to minister to her and bring hope. There's something so special about family, especially at Christmastime. We shop for each other, prepare special surprises to tickle the fancy of those we adore, and even create yummy dishes to bake, just to bring a smile to our loved ones' faces. All out of love. May we strive to be the "Elizabeths" to those, like Mary, who are troubled and confused.

• ◆ • ◆ •

I want to be like Elizabeth, Lord! Make me a safe place for people
to run to, not just during the holidays, but every day. I pray for
Your grace and mercy to shine through my eyes to others. Amen.

Unspeakable Gift

• ◆ ◆ •

Thank God for this gift too wonderful for words!
2 CORINTHIANS 9:15 NLT

Have you ever been so overwhelmed by an unexpected, over-the-top gift that you hardly knew how to respond? Perhaps tears sprang to your eyes because you simply couldn't come up with words to thank the giver. Their present, loaded with personal touches, was so well thought out that you were simply blown away. Who takes the time to bless someone that way? As wonderful as that gift might be, there's one that far surpasses it. It's a personalized gift, one with your name engraved on it. It will leave you speechless and alters your viewpoint forever. This gift is Jesus Christ, the Savior of the world. What does He ask you to do in response to such a gift? Accept Him and give Him rightful place in your heart.

• ◆ ◆ ◆ •

You sent the greatest gift of all, Father! Jesus, Savior of the world! Today I recommit myself to Him offering my heart as His home and His throne. Thank You for sending Your Son, Lord. Amen.

Forgiveness

• ◆ • ◆ •

God exalted him to his own right hand as Prince and Savior
that he might bring Israel to repentance and forgive their sins.
ACTS 5:31 NIV

Why is Christmas the season for forgiveness?
Because this is the time of year we're reminded of
God's greatest gift to mankind, that of His Son coming
to earth as a baby in a manger. Though the shepherds
and wise men couldn't have known it, they were gazing
into the eyes of the very One who would one day die in
their place on an old rugged cross. That cross represents
forgiveness for every sin we've ever committed. So, the
Christmas story is really a forgiveness story, for it's where
we first learn of God's gift. And it's a reminder that we
can forgive others, even when we don't feel like it.

• ◆ • ◆ •

Lord, I need to learn to forgive. May I learn from Your example.
Let this season be my teacher, Father. I'm grateful for the many
times You've forgiven me and I'm willing to admit that I
need Your help in this area of my life. Amen.

The Word Became Flesh

* ◆ ◆ ◆ *

In the beginning was the Word, and the Word was with God,
and the Word was God. The Word became flesh and made his
dwelling among us. We have seen his glory, the glory of the one
and only Son, who came from the Father, full of grace and truth.
JOHN 1:1, 14 NIV

It's so fascinating to think that Jesus (the Word) was/
is God, was *with* God in the very beginning (at
Creation) and then became flesh. Fascinating concept!
Jesus is the Word. And the Word took on flesh and
joined us here on planet earth for thirty-three and a half
years, God in human form. There's never been such a
remarkable story. When we think about Jesus being there
in the beginning of time, we are floored. He was there?
And He was here (on earth), too? And He's coming
again? What a miracle!

* ◆ ◆ ◆ *

Jesus, You were there! You were there at creation,
there in the stable, there on the cross, and there in my heart!
Everywhere I turn. . .You are! Thank You for taking on
flesh and coming to my rescue. I'm so grateful! Amen.

Humbled

• ◆ • ◆ •

And being found in appearance as a man, he humbled himself
by becoming obedient to death—even death on a cross!
PHILIPPIANS 2:8 NIV

Have you ever been humbled by a person or situation?
It's no fun, is it? There's a reason the word *humble*
makes up the first part of the word *humiliation*. On
the other hand, you can choose to humble yourself in
a given situation and not experience humiliation at all.
The difference is in the choosing. That's what Jesus did.
The God of heaven humbled Himself and chose—truly
chose—to come to earth as a babe. The humbling
continued as you examine the location of His birth: a
lowly stable. And again, He humbled Himself on the
cross at Calvary, taking our sin and shame, when He
didn't have to. Again, a choice. How wonderful, to see
that God chose to exalt Him, high above all earthly
kings. The very One who lowered Himself was elevated
by God. The same is true today. God continues to elevate
us as we bow the knee to Him. No humiliation. . .only
blessing!

• ◆ • ◆ •

Thanks for the reminder that humbling myself is a
good thing! You don't want to humiliate me, only to
see me make the right choices. I'm trying, Lord. Amen.

Save His People

. . ◆ . .

"She will bear a Son; and you shall call His name Jesus,
for He will save His people from their sins."
MATTHEW 1:21 NASB

If you've ever been in a frightening situation with
your family, you know what it's like to want to save
those you love. If a burglar came into your home or if
your car was propelled into a raging river, you would
do everything in your power to rescue those you were
with. Jesus had that same strategy: Save those I love. So
He gave no thought to His own life (picture yourself
jumping into the river to save your child) because love
propelled Him. Love will do that, you know. Jesus did far
more than risk His own life: He gave up the splendor of
heaven. And He wasn't coming to save our lives in the
physical sense; He came to save us from our sins. Like a
father jumping into a river to save his child, Christ leapt
from heaven. . .ready and willing to do anything and
everything to save His dying child.

. ◆ . ◆ .

Wow, Lord! You did all of that for me! You left everything
and came to save me. I'm so grateful, Father.
No one cares for me like You! Amen.

Fruit

• ◆ • ◆ •

A shoot will come up from the stump of Jesse;
from his roots a Branch will bear fruit.
ISAIAH 11:1 NIV

We read so much in the bible about bearing fruit. God wants us to be productive and to bring life to others. When we're fruitful, we give people something to chew on (pun intended). Jesus was our ultimate example of fruit-bearing. He taught us how to live. When we're faced with situations that seem nonsensical it's appropriate to ask the question: "What would Jesus do?" because His response should be our response, too. So, as you walk through this Christmas season, when you're struggling to respond to someone—or something—that strikes you the wrong way, remember Jesus, the ultimate fruit-bearer. He's waiting for you to follow His lead.

• ◆ • ◆ •

Lord, thank You for sending Your Son.
He was born to bear fruit, and so was I! May I
follow His example in all things, Father! Amen.

Free Gift

• ◆ • ◆ •

For the wages of sin is death, but the gift
of God is eternal life in Christ Jesus our Lord.
ROMANS 6:23 NIV

Have you ever gotten one of those not-quite-real checks in the mail? Maybe it's from a local car dealership, offering a $5000.00 discount toward the purchase of a car. Or maybe it's a $2000.00 check, good toward a $10,000.00 vacation to the Caribbean. These too-good-to-be-true gifts aren't really gifts at all, are they? They get your hopes up and then let you down in a hurry. Is there any such thing as a real free gift, one with no strings attached? One that seems too good to be true? Only in the person of Jesus Christ, who came as a baby wrapped in swaddling clothes. In that child, we find the only "free" gift that life has to offer.

• ◆ • ◆ •

Lord, thank You that the gift of Your Son was free! And He
came to free me from my sin, so the gift—and the result—
are both the same: free! Bless You again and again. Amen.

The Light Shines in Darkness

• ◆ ◆ ◆ •

In Him was life, and the life was the Light of men.
The Light shines in the darkness, and the
darkness did not comprehend it.
JOHN 1:4–5 NASB

Imagine yourself stepping outside in the wee hours of the night. The sky is dark and ominous. No stars in sight. Not even a shimmer from the moon. Then, bursting through the sky, a meteor, whizzing by. It lights the night sky and takes your breath away. It sheds light and causes you to gasp at its brilliance. That moment where the light hits the darkness is breathtaking, isn't it? So it must have been when the King of kings was born in the stable. How His light must've shimmered against the dark Bethlehem sky! How His brilliance must have awed those shepherds. What was the innkeeper thinking as people came and went, drawn by the light that hovered above the stable. What a majestic, radiant night!

• ◆ • ◆ •

Lord, I love Your light! It guides me and brings me comfort when I'm in a dark place. Thank You for the reminder that Your radiant light can illuminate every area of my life. I'm so grateful. Amen.

Every Good and Perfect Gift

• ◆ • ◆ •

Every good gift and every perfect gift is from above,
coming down from the Father of lights with whom
there is no variation or shadow due to change.
JAMES 1:17 ESV

Oh, the boxes under the tree! There are so many, and they're wrapped in a variety of different types of paper. From the outside, it's hard to tell what you might find, should you peek inside. But you know every one of them is special, not because of the wrapping, but because you know the giver. When a "giver" gives a gift, he or she does it out of love for the recipient. That's how it was when God gave the ultimate gift of His Son. Jesus didn't come wrapped in ribbons and bows, but He was given out of love. And, as we "unwrap" Him (make Him our Lord and Savior) we come to grips with the concept that this gift—God's Son—is truly the only perfect gift we'll ever receive.

• ◆ • ◆ •

Lord, Your Son is perfect! You sent nothing less than
the best for us because You love us. How we love You, too,
Father! What a great gift giver You are! Amen.

The Likeness of Men

• ◆ • ◆ •

You must have the same attitude that Christ Jesus had. Though
he was God, he did not think of equality with God as something
to cling to. Instead, he gave up his divine privileges; he took the
humble position of a slave and was born as a human being.
When he appeared in human form, he humbled himself in
obedience to God and died a criminal's death on a cross.
PHILIPPIANS 2:5–8 NLT

It's so hard to wrap our brains around the concept of
the Trinity: three in one. Father, Son, Holy Spirit.
Separate, yet together. Individual jobs, but one Lord.
And how fascinating, to think of Jesus, who didn't count
equality with the Father something to be grasped. What
was it like, then, to come to earth as a baby, to put a
human face on divinity. . .for all the world to see? For the
first time, the King of kings wore skin. And fingernails.
And toes. And looked at the world through human eyes.
And heard sounds through human ears. He tasted food
through a human mouth and digested food through a
human digestive tract. He became one of us. And yet,
in doing so, left none of His divinity behind. What a
remarkable God we serve!

• ◆ • ◆ •

Lord, You are truly remarkable. Three in one. Spirit. Flesh.
100% God. 100% human. How did You do it, Father?
I stand in awe of You, oh Lord! Amen.

God's Glory Revealed

• ◆ • ◆ •

"And the glory of the LORD will be revealed, and all people
will see it together. For the mouth of the LORD has spoken."
ISAIAH 40:5 NIV

In Old Testament times God revealed His glory in a
number of ways. To Moses, in the burning bush. To
Isaiah, in the temple. To the disciples, in far too many
ways to count! In all of the many ways the glory of God
had been revealed, no one had ever pictured the Lord's
holy presence hovering in and over a tiny stable, with
cattle nearby. And yet, in that holy place, the glory of
the Lord was revealed as never before. It was evident
in the eyes of a tiny baby boy and celebrated by all who
witnessed His coming. May we see the stable for what
it was and is: a holy place, a holy time, and a glory-filled
home for a King to dwell!

• ◆ • ◆ •

Lord, what a place for Your glory to be revealed. . .a humble stable.
And what a greater place still. . .the hearts of Your children!
Thank You for revealing Yourself to me, Father! Amen.

A Matter of the Heart

* ◆ * ◆ *

Above all else, guard your heart,
for everything you do flows from it.
PROVERBS 4:23 NIV

Perhaps there's no greater time than Christmas for us to guard our hearts. We have a tendency to get so wrapped up in the everyday "stuff" that we forget. We buy gifts out of rote. We get frustrated when we stand in line at the store behind the woman with a dozen coupons. We say we're in the giving spirit, but we're really just overwhelmed, feeling like we need to keep up with the Joneses. This season, take a moment to ask God to do a little heart surgery before the shopping and other festivities begin. He'll fine-tune your heart and give you the wherewithal to guard His work throughout the holiday season and beyond.

* ◆ * ◆ *

Lord, thank You for the reminder that You want me to guard
my heart. I open it to You, Father. Do Your work as the season
begins and help me protect it all year-round. Amen.

The Child Inside

• ◆ • ◆ •

And he said: "Truly I tell you, unless you change and become like little children, you will never enter the kingdom of heaven."
MATTHEW 18:3 NIV

Remember that childlike feeling that swept over you every Christmas? You couldn't wait for Christmas morning. The anticipation was almost too much! You watched with wonder as your parents set out cookies and milk for Santa. You stood in awe as snowflakes covered your windowpane. You couldn't sleep all night long as your imagination went into overdrive. What presents would you find under the tree? That same sense of anticipation can drive you, even now—not for material possessions, but in your walk with the Savior. He longs for you to lie awake at night, thinking of the many gifts He has given you. He loves it when you express your gratitude and your joy. Yes, you can be a child at heart. . . all of your life, no matter your age.

• ◆ • ◆ •

Lord, I'm so glad that You've reminded me to remain childlike in my faith. I remember what it was like, all those years ago, and I'm ready to feel that way again. Fill my heart with anticipation, Father. Amen.

Presents and Packages

• ◆ • ◆ •

Every good and perfect gift is from above,
coming down from the Father of the heavenly lights,
who does not change like shifting shadows.
JAMES 1:17 NIV

There's something so exciting about holding a wrapped gift in our hands, isn't there? Perhaps it's our curiosity getting the better of us. We want to know what's inside, underneath the ribbons and bows. We speculate, try to figure it out. How we hope it's something we will love! We're also mesmerized by gifts because they remind us how much we are loved by the giver. Whether it's a parent, spouse, child, or friend. . . someone took the time to lovingly select, wrap, and trim that precious gift. The very act reminds us that we are adored. Of course the greatest gift giver of all is the Lord. He sent His Son, the perfect present. No ribbons. No bows. No fancy paper. Just a babe, wrapped in swaddling clothes. Oh, but opening that gift and holding it close to our hearts can change everything.

• ◆ • ◆ •

What a present You are, Jesus! You're the best gift I've ever received,
not just at Christmastime, but all year-round. Thank You for
offering Your life for me. How can I express my gratitude? Amen.

Traditions Passed Down

• ◆ • ◆ •

Now I commend you because you remember me in everything
and maintain the traditions even as I delivered them to you.
1 CORINTHIANS 11:2 ESV

Did you ever stop to think about how traditions get started? Why do we eat certain foods on certain holidays? Why do we sing particular songs at Christmas or celebrate with a family meal at Easter? Many of these things are traditions, passed down from generations before us. Some traditions are silly, and have no real significance. They're just fun. Others are life changing. Gathering around the table during the holidays, for instance. Where else can we have our bellies and hearts filled simultaneously? Candlelight service on Christmas Eve. Waking up early on Christmas morning to read the Christmas story to the kids and then open gifts. What a holy, blessed time together as a family. Yes, some traditions are definitely worth passing on to future generations!

• ◆ • ◆ •

Lord, I don't want to do things out of rote, simply because
that's how we've always done them. But I do want to pass
down the "good stuff" to my children and grandchildren.
Show me the difference between the two, I pray. Amen.

The Passing of Years

• ◆ • ◆ •

But I trusted in thee, O LORD: I said, Thou art my God.
My times are in thy hand: deliver me from the hand
of mine enemies, and from them that persecute me.
PSALM 31:14–15 KJV

The years just seem to buzz by, don't they? One minute we're young. The next we're in our teens. Then, with just the blink of the proverbial eye, we're parents and grandparents. And we can't figure out how it all happened so quickly! No matter how many years we have in our lives, it's important to remember to have life in our years. This is especially true at Christmastime. We can be the life of the party—the one extending grace when others are fretting. The one with a generous heart when others aren't as giving. In other words, we can make every moment count.

• ◆ • ◆ •

Father, I'm so grateful for the years You've given me.
I don't want to waste a moment. May I be known
as the one who lives life to its fullest! Amen.

Affirming

* * ◆ *

*My son, be attentive to my words; incline your ear
to my sayings. Let them not escape from your sight;
keep them within your heart. For they are life to
those who find them, and healing to all their flesh.*
PROVERBS 4:20–22 ESV

People who take the time to offer affirmation are such a blessing. When others around us are criticizing, reminding us of our flaws, affirming people lift us up. They encourage and make us believe we are capable of great things. They're not looking out for themselves. They really do have our best interests at heart, so they can be trusted. Affirmation is truly one of the best gifts we can give during the Christmas season and year-round. May we lift others up with our words and offer them the gift of encouragement, with our words and our actions!

* ◆ * ◆ *

*Lord, I want to be an affirming person. What a lovely gift to offer
people during this hectic season. May my words be encouraging,
uplifting, and filled with grace, just as Yours are to me. Amen.*

R&R

• ◆ • ◆ •

By the seventh day God had finished the work he had been doing;
so on the seventh day he rested from all his work. And God
blessed the seventh day and made it holy, because on it he rested
from all the work of creating that he had done.
GENESIS 2:2–3 NIV

How we rush—from place to place, friendship to friendship, event to event. When we're on the go all of the time we don't have time to stop and reflect. We also don't have time to take care of our bodies, as God would ask. This is particularly true during the holiday season. We're so busy shopping, baking cookies, prepping our holiday dinner, wrapping gifts, that we sometimes forget the R&R (rest and relaxation) part. If we move too fast, if we don't get adequate rest, we'll crater by Christmas Day. So, pacing ourselves is best, and rest is essential. Don't believe it? Just ask the One who created you! Even He took one day off!

• ◆ • ◆ •

Lord, I'll admit it: Sometimes I forget to rest. I go, go,
go and don't relax. Thanks for the reminder that it's okay
to slow down, even during the Christmas season! Amen.

Blessing

• ◆ • ◆ •

"I will make you into a great nation and I will bless you;
I will make your name great, and you will be a blessing."
GENESIS 12:2 NIV

Think about the great men and women in the Old
Testament days. Oftentimes the fathers would
pass on their blessing—their legacy—to the oldest son.
That birthright would travel down from generation to
generation, a coveted gift. How wonderful it must have
been, to receive something so life changing. Did you
know it's still possible to pass on blessings, not just to
your children, but to those who love you? Every day
you can make up your mind to be a blessing to others.
Perhaps you'll start a chain event! The blessings will flow
from person to person, all season long.

• ◆ • ◆ •

Lord, thank You for the reminder that I have the opportunity
to bless others and start a chain reaction. That's my plan
this Christmas. . .to be a blessing to others. Amen.

End of Year

*Brothers and sisters, I do not consider myself yet to have taken hold
of it. But one thing I do: Forgetting what is behind and straining
toward what is ahead, I press on toward the goal to win the prize
for which God has called me heavenward in Christ Jesus.*
PHILIPPIANS 3:13–14 NIV

The close of the year is always such a bittersweet
time, isn't it? We have an opportunity to look back,
to see how far we've come. We reflect on the sad times
and celebrate the good. We remember those we've lost
and enjoy those who remain. As you face the end of the
year, remember to take some time to look back, but don't
linger there. We don't live in the past. Shift your gaze to
the future, to the New Year. The possibilities are endless,
and God's joy is set before you.

• ◆ • ◆ •

*I don't want to spend too much time looking back, Lord, but I am
grateful for the blessings You've poured out over the past year.
Thank You for walking with me every step of the way. Amen.*

The Reason for the Season

. ◆ . ◆ .

*"For today in the city of David there has been
born for you a Savior, who is Christ the Lord."*
LUKE 2:11 NASB

Christmastime is sheer bliss for some, agony for others.
Many get in the holiday spirit weeks ahead of time,
and hit the malls, pocketbooks in hand, to buy, buy,
buy. Others hide their heads under the covers and try
to forget the season altogether. No cookie baking. No
parties. Nothing. No matter where you stand on holiday
celebrations, do your best to put Christmas in its rightful
place this year. Keep your focus on Jesus, the reason for
the season. (That's more than just a saying, after all!)
If you make up your mind to celebrate Him—truly
celebrate Him—then this Christmas has the potential to
be your best ever!

. ◆ . ◆ .

*I choose to remember the real reason for the season, Lord!
It's all about the Christ Child, not about superfluous stuff.
May I never forget that, without that babe in the manger,
there would be no cause for celebration! Amen.*

Holidays and Holy Days

• ◆ • ◆ •

*Nehemiah said, "Go and enjoy choice food and sweet drinks,
and send some to those who have nothing prepared. This day is holy
to our Lord. Do not grieve, for the joy of the LORD is your strength."*
NEHEMIAH 8:10 NIV

People get so bent out of shape during the Christmas
season. They debate the phrases "Merry Christmas"
and "Happy Holidays." Arguments ensue over which
should be used. It's awesome to remember that Christmas is about the coming of Christ, but the word *holidays*
has spiritual significance, too. *Holi-* means "holy," after
all. The key here is to keep the holy in our holidays, to
remember that the Christmas season is, indeed, a holy,
spiritual season. It's all about Him, after all, not us! So,
Happy Holidays *and* Merry Christmas! And may our
response to all be one of good cheer.

• ◆ • ◆ •

*Lord, I'm so grateful for this holy season. What a sweet time
to celebrate Your Son's birth. No matter how people greet me,
I'll respond with love and peace. May You be blessed! Amen.*

Relationships

• ◆ • ◆ •

Walk with the wise and become wise,
for a companion of fools suffers harm.
PROVERBS 13:20 NIV

Relationships can be tough any time of year, but especially during the holidays. Tempers flare, feelings get hurt, and everything feels exaggerated. That's why it's more important than ever to guard your heart during the Christmas season. Guard your relationships, too. Keep a distance from those who would stir up trouble and hang tight with those who encourage and uplift. Don't get drawn into unnecessary drama (tough, for sure!) and remember to ask God to lead and guide, no matter what—or who—you're facing. Most of all, lean on God for wisdom and ask Him to surround you with people who will make you strong.

• ◆ • ◆ •

I want to follow Your leading, Lord! May I be
surrounded by wise people during the holiday season.
I want to walk in Your ways. . .always. Amen.

Cookies and Cocoa

• ◆ • ◆ •

Two are better than one, because they
have a good reward for their toil.
ECCLESIASTES 4:9 ESV

Did you ever wonder why people always feel they should have cookies and cocoa during the Christmas season? There's nothing like warm, sweet cocoa to make a person feel better after time out in the cold. Sipping that frothy goodness brings warmth and comfort and conjures up happy memories of childhood. And cookies? Why, grandmothers across the globe await Christmastime so that they can pass on their recipes and decorating skills to grandchildren. There's no greater time to share "in the kitchen" time than Christmas. So, the next time you take a swig of cocoa or nibble on a Christmas cookie, remember. . .you're creating memories.

• ◆ • ◆ •

Lord, I love the memories I'm making with my family during
the holidays. Whether they're in the kitchen, around the table,
or with a cup of cocoa in hand, it's all about the people I'm with
(and I'm grateful for them). Amen.

A Joyful Noise

• ◆ • ◆ •

Make a joyful noise unto the LORD, all the earth:
make a loud noise, and rejoice, and sing praise.
PSALM 98:4 KJV

Christmas is a noisy season! All of that caroling,
rushing about at the mall, fussing at kids not to peek
at presents, hollering at the dog not to chew up the gifts
under the tree, and rehearsing the Christmas play at
church. . .whew! Talk about loud! But what better season
to make a joyful noise than Christmas? May our voices
be raised in joyful song at what God has done.
We celebrate. . .loudly. . .the gift of the Savior. With
every carol, every family visit, every cookie baked, we
praise the King for His goodness. He's worthy of our
praise, no matter how loud. (And boy, can it get loud!)

• ◆ • ◆ •

Lord, You are worthy of praise, all year-round! I choose to celebrate
this Christmas by making a joyful noise. No matter what's going
on around me, my heart is dedicated to You, Lord. Amen.

Helping the Less Fortunate

• ◆ • ◆ •

"For there will never cease to be poor in the land.
Therefore I command you, 'You shall open wide your hand
to your brother, to the needy and to the poor, in your land.'"
DEUTERONOMY 15:11 ESV

We've all heard the expression: "He's down on his luck." All around us people are hurting. So let's go out of our way this Christmas to help those less fortunate. Here are some fun ideas: Volunteer to serve Thanksgiving or Christmas dinner at a homeless shelter. Make scarves (as part of a goody package) to give the homeless. While you're baking for your own family, prepare extra plates of goodies for elderly friends and neighbors. Encourage your children to give a gift for every one they receive (from their stash of existing toys, perhaps). There are so many ways to make the holidays fun for everyone, even those who are going through hard times.

• ◆ • ◆ •

Lord, thank You for giving me creative ideas. I can't wait to
implement them. Show me who You want me to bless, Father,
and I'll enjoy every minute of surprising them with Your love. Amen.

Creativity

*"You have many workers: stonecutters, masons and carpenters,
as well as those skilled in every kind of work in gold and
silver, bronze and iron—craftsmen beyond number.
Now begin the work, and the LORD be with you."*
1 CHRONICLES 22:15–16 NIV

We are created in the image of a creative God, and there's no better time than Christmas to celebrate that fact. Are you low on funds this year? Then "craft" your Christmas gifts. Make scrapbooks or other hand-made presents. Wondering how you can feed a large crew? Get creative! Have a Mexican potluck dinner instead of your usual Christmas fare. Wondering how you can pay for tickets to see *The Nutcracker*? Go to a community theater production instead of a professional one. There are all sorts of ways to have fun without breaking the bank, if you use your God-given creativity! 'Tis the season. . .to get creative!

*Lord, I'm so glad You created me in Your image! I love being
creative. Give me fresh, new ideas this Christmas, Father.
I can't wait to see what You have up Your sleeve. Amen.*

God's Holy Plan

• ◆ • ◆ •

The heart of man plans his way,
but the LORD establishes his steps.
PROVERBS 16:9 ESV

Oh, how we love to plan. We set those plans in motion, oftentimes without asking God His opinion. On and on we go, especially at Christmastime. We buzz from here to there, determined and frantic. This year, let's slow down a bit and ask for God's plans instead of our own. He longs for us to do things His way, after all. And when we're walking according to His will, things will go smoothly (and we won't have to run over anyone along the way to get what we want). Now, there's a lovely idea, and not just during the holidays!

• ◆ • ◆ •

It's all about You, Lord! Your plan. Your thoughts. Your will.
I'm so grateful that You whisper Your instructions to my heart.
May I stay at the very center of Your will, so that I'm always
walking according to Your plan. Amen.

Traveling

• ◆ • ◆ •

"Let us pass through your country. We will stay on the
main road; we will not turn aside to the right or to the left."
DEUTERONOMY 2:27 NIV

During the holiday season roads are filled with
travelers. Folks are headed to Grandma's house,
Great-aunt Maggie's, or perhaps to the in-laws. The idea
of flying or driving during the Christmas season can be
stressful, but it doesn't have to be if you look at it as an
adventure. Why not put together a journal that everyone
in the family can contribute to? That way, you'll have it to
read next Christmas, and the one after. And while you're
at it, let the kids help with travel plans. They will enjoy
it and might just come up with some alternate routes to
make the journey a real adventure.

• ◆ • ◆ •

Lord, I'm grateful for modern transportation. Cars. Planes.
Subways. These are all things we take for granted, Father.
At least we're not traveling by donkey or covered wagon!
Thank You for making this year's Christmas travels an
adventure we can all remember. Amen.

Respect for Elders

· ◆ · ◆ ·

*"You shall stand up before the gray head and honor the face
of an old man, and you shall fear your God: I am the LORD."*
LEVITICUS 19:32 ESV

*W*e're called to honor our elders all year long. The
Christmas season gives us ample opportunity
to do just that because it often places us in situations
with those who are older than us. What a lovely time
to remind our children of the importance of treating
grandparents, elderly aunts and uncles, and other
relatives with the respect they deserve. And while we're
at it, why not give the children a little nudge to ask their
elders specific questions like, "What was Christmas like
when you were my age, Grandma?" or "What was your
favorite Christmas present ever, Grandpa?" This will stir
up a fun conversation, for sure!

· ◆ · ◆ ·

*Lord, thank You for the reminder that we are to treat our
elders with the respect they deserve. Give our family creative
ideas this Christmas, so that everyone feels included. Amen.*

Self-Control

• ◆ • ◆ •

Like a city whose walls are broken
through is a person who lacks self-control.
PROVERBS 25:28 NIV

God longs for us to be alert and self-controlled. This is critical, no matter the time of year, but especially important during the Christmas season! Sometimes we forget. We spend as though we have money (when we do not) and we stay busy, busy, busy, ignoring the things that really matter. Self-control begins by acknowledging that you have a problem. From there, it's great to make lists and set goals. Be realistic. And remember, Christmas won't last forever, but good judgment will!

• ◆ • ◆ •

Lord, I want to make good decisions, not just during the holidays,
but year-round. Please help me when I feel like I'm losing control.
I want to be generous, Father, but within reason! When I'm slipping
over the edge, please draw me back by Your Spirit, I pray. Amen.

Our Gift to the World

* ◆ * ◆ *

He came as a witness to testify concerning that light,
so that through him all might believe.
JOHN 1:7 NIV

During the Christmas season we focus so much on gifts—the things we give others and the things we receive. Perhaps it's time to start thinking of the gifts we can give the world. How can we make an impact for the Kingdom of God in the coming year? On Social Media? In our work relationships? In our community? God wants us to be a powerful witness, and we can be. Our words in passing, our comments on social media sites. . . all of these things can be a gift to others. We must make up our minds to give, give, give, not take, take, take. Our posts must be others-directed, as much as possible. We can give the gift of Bible verses, song lyrics, and so on. We can link people to hopeful testimonies and stories. In doing so, we pull the focus from "Me, myself, and I" to those who need to hear a message of hope. In other words, we give the gift of Jesus!

* ◆ * ◆ *

Lord, this season, my greatest desire is to share
Your love with others. Help me daily, I pray. Amen.

Christ, the Center

• ◆ ◆ ◆ •

He is before all things,
and in him all things hold together.
COLOSSIANS 1:17 NIV

Have you ever pondered the word *center* before? The center of an object is its safest place, the point of balance. It's where the eye travels first. When you're driving a car, you want to keep your eyes on the center of what's in front of you, not wandering off to the right or left. The same is true of the Christmas season. When we keep Jesus at the center—not just in the manger as some sort of made-up fairy tale—but in the very center of our hearts and lives, everything else will be in balance. Relationship woes, financial problems, busy schedules. . . these all come into alignment with Christ at the center. So don't lose your focus this season. Let your eye (and your heart) travel to where it needs to be.

• ◆ ◆ ◆ •

Lord, may I keep my eyes on You this season. I know what it's
like to be out of balance and I don't want that, especially with
so many things on my plate. So keep me centered, Father! Amen.

Empty Boxes

• ◆ • ◆ •

"Let him not trust in emptiness, deceiving himself,
for emptiness will be his payment."
JOB 15:31 ESV

*U*nwrapping presents is a blast, but, oh. . .the mess that follows! Torn bits of paper cover the floor, along with ribbons, bows, nametags, and other shredded bits of boxes and whatnot. Talk about a mess! At this stage of the game, it's tempting to look around at all of the empty packages and empty boxes and feel a little. . . empty. It's that same feeling a mother gets after she's given birth: after-birth blues. All of that anticipation and then, in an instant, it's over. So now what? How do you fill that empty space inside? By acknowledging that the Savior is alive and well and enthroned upon your heart. He's got great plans for you in the coming year. So shed those empty feelings. There's a great road ahead.

• ◆ • ◆ •

I'm so grateful You are with me, even when the festivities
are over, Lord. Thank You for Your presence. Amen.

Financial Debt

• ◆ • ◆ •

"Give, and it will be given to you. They will pour into your lap a
good measure, pressed down, shaken together, and running over.
For by your standard of measure it will be measured to you in return."
LUKE 6:38 NASB

It's fun to spend money at Christmastime, but only if you actually have money. It's a lot less fun to use credit cards and get the bills in January. Whoa! Talk about a downer. And the added stress will take away from the joy of the season, for sure! That's why we need a better plan. Learning to live within your means is God's will, and not just during the holidays. So guard your spending. Plan ahead and set aside funds so that you can buy those gifts, but do so with a guarded mind and heart. The kids won't know the difference, but your pocketbook will!

• ◆ • ◆ •

Please help me budget, Lord. I don't want to get in over my head.
Thank You for the reminder that buying "stuff" isn't important.
Living a balanced life is. Amen.

Whimsy

• ◆ • ◆ •

*"He will yet fill your mouth with laughter,
and your lips with shouting."*
JOB 8:21 ESV

There's no time like Christmas to be filled with whimsy. Silly songs. Goofy traditions. Favorite wacky movies. Yes, there's something about the holiday season that brings out the whimsical in us. . .and that's okay! We are created in the image of a creative God, after all, and whimsy goes along with that. So don't be afraid to embrace your inner child this season. Act out the Christmas play. Sing at the top of your lungs. Start new, silly traditions. Go for it. . .and have a blast every step of the way!

• ◆ • ◆ •

*Oh, how I love to be childlike at Christmastime, Lord.
Thank You for reminding me that whimsy is fine,
not just during the holidays, but all year long. Amen.*

Hospitality

• ◆ • ◆ •

Be hospitable to one another without complaint.
1 PETER 4:9 NASB

Don't you love those folks who have a gift for hospitality? They open their homes to others, feed them choice foods, offer them sweet conversation, and do it all with grace and ease. Or so it seems. If there's one thing we need during the holiday season, it's this very special gift—anointing, if you will—to be hospitable to others. May they find our homes welcoming, our conversation encouraging, our foods tantalizing (as much as we are able) and most of all, our hearts available. Perhaps hospitality will be the great gift you give someone this year. And just think. . .you don't even have to wrap it up!

• ◆ • ◆ •

Lord, I want to be known as someone who is hospitable. I don't want to keep my door closed because I'm ashamed of my house or my inability to cook. This isn't about keeping up with the Joneses. . .it's about sharing my heart and home with others. Help me, I pray. Amen.

The Gift of Time

• ◆ • ◆ •

Your love has given me great joy and encouragement, because you,
brother, have refreshed the hearts of the Lord's people.
PHILEMON 1:7 NIV

Sometimes we give gifts in place of time. This happens year-round: The absent father gives his children exorbitant gifts for birthday or Christmas to make up for the fact that they rarely see him. The workaholic mother spoils her children with gifts because she's unable to give them what they really need and want: her time. Perhaps there's no greater season to reflect on the gift of time than Christmas. We need to slow down, take a deep breath, and figure out ways to give t-i-m-e to those in our immediate circle. This might take some doing, so pull out your calendar, go over your schedule, and pencil in time with those you love.

• ◆ • ◆ •

Lord, sometimes I wish there were more than twenty-four
hours in a day. Then, just as quickly, I'm glad there aren't!
I'm tired enough already. Please show me how I can give
more time to those I love this Christmas season. Amen.

Fellowship

• ◆ • ◆ •

Iron sharpens iron,
and one man sharpens another.
PROVERBS 27:17 ESV

Picture this: It's Christmas Day. Food is cooked and ready to be served. . .all but the Christmas ham, which needs to be sliced. You reach for a knife, but it's dull. Very dull. You're not able to slice through the meat, in fact. A dull knife is a useless knife. In order to be effective, it must be sharpened. The same is true with our friendships. We grow dull, if we're not careful, so we lean on our friends to "sharpen us up." It's not always easy (the sharpening process rarely is) but the effect is glorious! Like that knife, we're much more effective when we're sharp.

• ◆ • ◆ •

I get it, Lord! You're using my friends (their remarks,
their kindnesses, their grace, and their chastisements) to sharpen me
up. It helps to know that the work will have a positive result. Amen.

Conspiracy of Love

• ◆ • ◆ •

We know what love is because Christ gave His life for us.
We should give our lives for our brothers.
1 John 3:16 nlv

Have you ever "conspired" to love someone? Perhaps it's time! There's no better season than Christmas for conspiring, after all! Perhaps you could choose someone who's lonely or feels left out. Create a plan to make this person feel special during the holidays. Or maybe you could focus on someone who's difficult, who is tough to be around. Sending sweet notes or a special gift might be in order to bring down the walls. Regardless, the Lord will show you who to "target" if you ask. He's great at love conspiracies, after all. He lavishes that love on us every day, whether we deserve it or not.

• ◆ • ◆ •

Father, I want to be known as a love-lavisher. Show me who needs
a special dose of heavenly love this Christmas, and then give me
creative ideas, so that my conspiracy is really Your conspiracy. Amen.

Sugar on Top

• ◆ • ◆ •

"By their fruit you will recognize them. Do people pick grapes from thorn bushes, or figs from thistles?"
MATTHEW 7:16 NIV

Remember that little phrase you used as a kid when you were begging for something. "Please, please! With a little sugar on top!" The "sugar on top" part was your way of saying, "I'll love you forever and ever if you do this for me!" God wants us to put "sugar on top" even when there's nothing coming our way. When the person you love doesn't respond in kind, offer sugar on top. When a relative refuses to show up for Christmas dinner because she's angry at her sister, offer sugar on top. When you're waiting in line to pay for Christmas gifts. . .well, you get the idea. There's enough bitterness during the Christmas season. We could all stand a little extra sugar.

• ◆ • ◆ •

Lord, it's not always easy to add sugar on top, especially with everyone so rushed and harried during the Christmas season. But I'm going to give it my best shot. With Your help, I know I can do this. Amen.

Provision

• ◆ • ◆ •

I will bless her with abundant provisions;
her poor I will satisfy with food.
PSALM 132:15 NIV

*a*t every step in the Christmas story, God made provision for Mary and Joseph. When Mary received
the news, she received confirmation through her cousin,
Elizabeth. When Joseph was troubled, he received
confirmation through an angel. When the couple
traveled to Bethlehem and found no inn, they received
a temporary dwelling place in the stable. God even
provided guests (shepherds), to visit. And then of course,
God provided for Mary, Joseph, and the young boy, Jesus,
by sending the wise men with gifts of gold, frankincense,
and myrrh. How fascinating, to think through this story,
all the way to the cross. There, on Golgotha's hill, the
baby Jesus, now grown, continued to provide for all of
mankind by offering Himself as a sacrifice for sin. The
gifts just kept coming! From there, God sent His Spirit!

• ◆ • ◆ •

This season, as I give my gifts, I'm so mindful of Your provision,
Lord! Not only do You meet my material needs, You pour
Yourself out for me as an offering. I'm so grateful! Amen.

De-Grinching

• ◆ • ◆ •

Do all things without grumbling or disputing, that you
may be blameless and innocent, children of God without
blemish in the midst of a crooked and twisted generation,
among whom you shine as lights in the world.
PHILIPPIANS 2:14–15 ESV

All Dr. Seuss fans know who the Grinch is. He's that mean-spirited fellow with the sour disposition who ruins Christmas. Though he is an exaggerated character, we all know real-life people who seem a little too Grinch-like. You tell them the sky is blue; they counter that it's gray. You sing a happy song; they tell you the music hurts their ears. Living with (and around) Grinches is tough, particularly at Christmastime. But this is the best time of year to extend grace. It's not just a matter of appeasing the grumpy folks; it's an opportunity to minister God's love in the hopes that the person will change. Don't give up on the Grinches in your world. They're God's kids, too, after all.

• ◆ • ◆ •

Lord, I'll admit it's not easy to love the Grinches in my life
but I commit to give it my best shot this season. I'm going
to need Your help every step of the way, Father! Amen.

Snowflakes

• ◆ • ◆ •

I praise you, for I am fearfully and wonderfully made.
Wonderful are your works; my soul knows it very well.
PSALM 139:14 ESV

Rarely do we consider the role of the individual snowflake. We're too busy plowing mounds of snow to think about the individual flakes. Oh, but if we took the time to look, if we examined each little flake, we would find uniqueness. Did you know that God celebrates uniqueness? He loves diversity, which is why no snowflakes—or human beings—are created to be exactly alike. So, as you look at those white mounds of snow this year, think about the fact that God created you to be different from those around you. You're a beautiful snowflake!

• ◆ • ◆ •

Lord, I needed the reminder that it's okay to be different.
Sometimes I don't feel like those in my circle. We're all so. . .unique.
But that's okay, Father! I love the fact that You created me to be
an individual, not a cookie-cutter. Thank You for that. Amen.

Winter Wonderland

• ◆ • ◆ •

"As the rain and the snow come down from heaven,
and do not return to it without watering the earth
and making it bud and flourish, so that it yields seed for
the sower and bread for the eater, so is my word that goes
out from my mouth: It will not return to me empty, but will
accomplish what I desire and achieve the purpose for which I sent it."
ISAIAH 55:10–11 NIV

There's nothing more beautiful than a winter wonderland, especially at Christmastime. Most everyone dreams of a white Christmas, after all. Of course, weather delays at airports, mounds of icky gray snow on the edge of the driveway, and shivering children with coughs and cold might damper the holiday spirit, but we can make up our minds to keep spirits bright. And if we live in areas that see no snow, we can always make our own winter wonderland, by decorating with a winter theme. So bring on the hot chocolate! Build those snowmen. Let's settle in for a Christmas season that puts everyone in mind of a winter wonderland!

• ◆ • ◆ •

Thank You for my imagination, Lord. Even when it's not
snowing outside, I can imagine a winter wonderland. May our
spirits be bright, no matter what the weather holds. Amen.

Christmas Cards

• ◆ • ◆ •

You yourselves are our letter, written on our hearts,
known and read by everyone.
2 CORINTHIANS 3:2 NIV

Have you ever wondered why Christmas cards are sent? The custom was started in the mid-1800s by a fellow who wanted to see the postal service used by ordinary people. By the late 1800s people of all economic levels were joining in the fun. Sharing your thoughts through a lovely card just adds more joy to an already festive season. It serves as a reminder to the recipient that they haven't been forgotten: They're still loved, still in the loop. And they are good for the sender, too! Adding addresses to those envelopes reminds us of just how blessed we are. God has surrounded us with wonderful friends.

• ◆ • ◆ •

What joy, Father! I get to send and receive messages of love to
those in my circle. Thank You for giving me the opportunity
to share Your message of love through a little card. Amen.

Taking Care of the Neighbors

• ◆ ◆ ◆ •

"The second is this: 'You shall love your neighbor as yourself.'
There is no other commandment greater than these."
MARK 12:31 ESV

Don't you love to surprise people? It's sheer delight, to do the unexpected. What joy, to give when people don't anticipate it! This is a lot of fun where neighbors are concerned. This Christmas season, why not pray for creative ideas to bless the people on your right and left, or that neighbor across the street. Maybe you're particularly fond of an elderly couple down the block. Perhaps a gift card is in order, or bags of groceries to help them prepare for their Christmas dinner? The possibilities are endless. Just ask the Lord to guide. . . and He surely will!

• ◆ ◆ ◆ •

Father, I love to surprise people. Show me who to bless. . .
and how. I want to be known as a giver, Lord, not just
in my family, but to my neighbors as well. Amen.

Please Come Home for Christmas

· ◆ · ◆ ·

*The LORD will watch over your coming
and going both now and forevermore.*
PSALM 121:8 NIV

*W*e've all heard the expression, "Home is where the heart is." For most, that is the case. There's a yearning to be back home for the holidays. Others, though, don't feel as welcome at home, so they shy away. Years become decades, decades become lifetimes. If your family is going through a tough season with walls of separation up between the members, then hit your knees in prayer. Ask God for His perspective. Before you cry out, "Please come home for Christmas," pray the words, "Lord, may they come home to You, so that they will enjoy coming home to us."

· ◆ · ◆ ·

*Lord, I get it! You want Your children to come home to You,
and not just during the holidays. As much as we want our
families together, You want it even more. Give me an
eternal perspective, Father! Amen.*

Plugged In

● ◆ ◆ ◆ ●

The people which sat in darkness saw great light; and to them which sat in the region and shadow of death light is sprung up.
MATTHEW 4:16 KJV

Christmas is a season of light. All around us, the Christmas lights twinkle—on houses and city buildings. All of those lights depend on one thing: electricity. And electricity wouldn't do them a bit of good if not for another thing: plugs. All of those lights must be plugged in to the source. In the same way, we have to stay plugged into Jesus, the reason for the season, if we're going to make it through the ups and downs of the Christmas holiday season. We can't let the distractions unplug us (though they tug at us from every side). If we stay hooked up to the source, we'll have the power to light up the lives of all who come in contact with us. What a lovely idea!

● ◆ ◆ ◆ ●

Father, may I stay plugged in to You! I need Your power, Lord. I need Your light. Please keep me from distractions so that I might shine brightly. Amen.

Children Laughing

• ◆ • ◆ •

*Then our mouth was filled with laughter, and our tongue
with shouts of joy; then they said among the nations,
"The LORD has done great things for them."*
PSALM 126:2 ESV

The sound of children's laughter is like music to the ears, (most of the time, anyway). This is especially true at Christmastime. They find such delight in every little thing: gingerbread houses, Christmas lights, hand-made ornaments, cookie baking, cupcake-making, and (of course) present-opening. Nothing lights up a room more than a child's sound of glee when a gift they've been hoping for is revealed. Parents around the globe love that sound. So do grandparents. So let the joy ring out. Let the laughter peal across the house, (even if the noise makes you a little crazy at times).

• ◆ • ◆ •

*Lord, I love the sound of Your children's laughter.
What joy! And there's no better time than right now,
Christmas, to celebrate the joy they bring. Amen.*

Hustle and Bustle

• ◆ ◆ ◆ •

Very early in the morning, while it was still dark, Jesus got up,
left the house and went off to a solitary place, where he prayed.
MARK 1:35 NIV

Wow, Christmas can be crazy! Ten people in line
ahead of you at the grocery store. No available
parking spaces at the super center. Grumpy bosses,
frazzled spouses, and kids who won't stop saying, "Can
I get *this* for Christmas?" as they point at the latest,
greatest gadget. The season of our Savior's birth was
never meant to be stressful. Just the opposite, in fact. So,
if you find yourself overwhelmed, take a deep breath and
remind yourself why you're celebrating in the first place.
Re-focus your heart, your thoughts, and your prayers, to
be Christ-centered. Then, when complications and chaos
arise (and they surely will), you will be better prepared to
deal with them.

• ◆ ◆ ◆ •

Lord, I don't want this season to be chaotic. I want
to celebrate the wonder of You! So, calm my heart,
squelch the anxiety, and bring peace and rest, I pray. Amen.

Overflowing

· ◆ · ◆ ·

Honor the LORD *with your wealth, with the firstfruits of
all your crops; then your barns will be filled to overflowing,
and your vats will brim over with new wine.*
PROVERBS 3:9–10 NIV

Have you ever overfilled a coffee cup? What a waste
of great coffee! As it runs down the sides of the cup,
spilling over onto the counter below, you sigh and reach
for a napkin to clean up the mess. Oh, but God wants
us to live an overflowing life! In our hearts, our spirits,
and even our attitudes. He wants us to be so filled with
Him that we spill over onto our family, our coworkers,
and our neighbors. There's truly no better season than
Christmas to experiment with an overflowing lifestyle!
Open yourself to the possibilities and watch as God
supernaturally spills your joy onto all of those around you.

· ◆ · ◆ ·

*I want to overflow, Lord, with Your goodness, Your strength,
Your joy, and Your love! I give You full reign to "spill"
me onto those in my path. Amen.*

A Sign

* ◆ * ◆ *

"Therefore the Lord himself will give you a sign: The virgin will conceive and give birth to a son, and will call him Immanuel."
ISAIAH 7:14 NIV

The sign industry is a pretty impressive industry. It's amazing what businesses will spend on a sign, so they can attract customers. Whether it's for hamburgers or shoes or designer paint, proprietors want to be found. They want potential patrons to come into their stores and spend money. That won't happen unless the business can be easily located and identified.

The same is true for our roads and landmarks. The government doesn't want travelers stopping at every bend in the road to ask for directions, so they display clear signs to keep people from getting lost.

God wants people to find Christ. He wanted the shepherds and the wise men to find Him, so He gave them a clear sign. He wants each of us to find Christ as well. And though Christ is no longer a baby in a manger, He is still very real. When we seek Him, God will provide the signs we need, along with clear directions to His presence.

◆ * ◆ * ◆

Lord, help me to always find You,
no matter what situation I'm in. Amen.

Peace Within

• ◆ • ◆ •

The LORD gives strength to his people;
the LORD blesses his people with peace.
PSALM 29:11 NIV

We hear so much about peace on earth during the Christmas season. And it's true, we do need to pray for peace on earth, especially now, with so much turmoil around the globe. But real peace, lasting peace, begins in the heart. If we aren't at peace (internally) then our actions will never be peaceful. We'll be knee-jerking all of the time if we're wound up on the inside. So this year, instead of just praying for peace on earth, pray for peace in the hearts of men. Start with those closest to you—family, friends, neighbors, and so on—and then watch as God uses peaceful hearts to transform the world.

• ◆ • ◆ •

Lord, please start with me! Bring peace to my heart instead of
turmoil. May my actions be just that. . .actions, and not reactions.
May I start a movement of peace in my world. Amen.

Goodwill to Men

* ◆ * ◆ *

Glory to God in the highest, and on
earth peace, good will toward men.
LUKE 2:14 KJV

What does it mean to have good will toward men? We know, of course, that we're to treat each other well to wish others the best. We're to live by the Golden Rule. But if we really study the words of the angels in various translations, we might also discover that these words lend themselves to God's good will toward *us*, His children, in sending this amazing gift—the Christ Child. With hands extended from heaven, God offered us peace, lasting peace, not just for the generation that actually saw Jesus with their eyes, but for all who would one day know Him as Lord and Savior. What favor God bestowed through this precious gift!

* ◆ * ◆ *

Father, thank You for Jesus, the gift of peace. Through Him,
we can have lasting peace in our hearts that extends to others.
This is how we live out the Golden Rule: by loving You first,
and others second. I'm so grateful, Lord. Amen.

Budgeting

Moreover, it is required of stewards
that they be found faithful.
1 CORINTHIANS 4:2 ESV

Many people dread budgeting, especially at Christmastime, but it doesn't have to be a chore. In fact, if you're creative you can plan for your holiday shopping months in advance. Many people start setting aside money in January, putting it in a special account, meant just for Christmas gifts. Others use a layaway system. Still others budget a specific amount per person. The point is that you don't have to bankrupt yourself to give. Coming up short the week after Christmas is no fun, after all. And look for ways to give less expensive gifts, or even offer services, such as foot massages, babysitting, or things like that. Guard that pocketbook, but have a blast!

Lord, I don't want Christmas to be about money;
I want it to be about You. Please give me a solid plan
so that my shopping list isn't overwhelming. I want
to be a good steward of what You've given me. Amen.

Parties

• ◆ • ◆ •

So, whether you eat or drink,
or whatever you do, do all to the glory of God.
1 CORINTHIANS 10:31 ESV

The party lovers of the world really enjoy the
holiday season. They look for every opportunity
to spend time with friends and loved ones. Ornament
exchanges. Sunday school parties. The office Christmas
party. Gatherings with family members. . .they love it
all! Celebrating the season is a lot of fun, but the best
party of all is the one that goes on in our hearts when
we realize the significance of what God did for us 2000
years ago. When we're filled with joy on the inside, it's
much easier to celebrate on the outside. It's time to make
Christmas a party from the inside-out!

• ◆ • ◆ •

Lord, I love to have fun. I enjoy being with others. But I'm more
grateful for the party inside of my heart as I ponder the reality
of Your love and sacrifice for me. How blessed I am. Amen.

Meet Me in the Stable

• ◆ • ◆ •

Honor and majesty surround him;
strength and joy fill his dwelling.
1 CHRONICLES 16:27 NLT

Can you imagine what it must have been like in that stable? The presence of the Lord had never been— and will never be—as real as it was in that holy place. Even though we'll never know exactly what Mary and Joseph must have felt as they held the Savior in their arms, we have a glimpse of that glory every time we step into our prayer closets and spend time with the Lord. Just as He did in days of old, the King of kings invites us to the stable, a precious meeting place, to gaze into His eyes and ponder His magnificence.

• ◆ • ◆ •

Lord, so many times I've wondered what it must've been like that
amazing night as Mary and Joseph gazed into their baby's eyes for
the first time. Thank You for inviting me into the stable with You,
Father. I'm honored to meet You there. Amen.

In Touch

• ◆ • ◆ •

"I give you a new command: Love each other. You must
love each other as I have loved you. All people will
know that you are my followers if you love each other."
JOHN 13:34–35 NCV

It seems the year just whizzes by. Winter buzzes into
spring and before you can blink an eye, summer
has arrived in all its glory. Just as quickly, it's time for
school to start again. And, moments later, stores begin
to stock their shelves for. . .you guessed it. . .Christmas!
Because things are so often in a whirl, we often don't
always get to spend quality time with those we love.
Things are just moving too fast. That's one reason why
Christmas is extra special, because it puts us back in
touch with those we've been missing. There's nothing
like a cup of cocoa, a few cookies, and an ornament
exchange party to bring friends together, after all.

• ◆ • ◆ •

I'm so grateful for time with those I love, Lord. Even though
I don't get to spend as much quality time with friends as I'd like,
Christmas always seems to bring us together. Thank You
for this precious season. Amen.

Christmas Every Day

• ◆ • ◆ •

You have enlarged the nation and increased their joy;
they rejoice before you as people rejoice at the harvest,
as warriors rejoice when dividing the plunder.
ISAIAH 9:3 NIV

Perhaps you know people who celebrate Christmas in July. They deck the halls while turning on the air conditioner. It's great fun to realize that Christmas is as much a way of thinking as a particular day. When we're focused on God, keeping our eyes on His plan, we really do keep a piece of Christmas in our hearts, no matter the season. Isn't that what Christmas is all about, anyway. . . taking time away from the busyness of life to focus on the One who came to give His life for us? If that's the case, then let's celebrate in the springtime, too. . .and the fall! He's worthy of our praise, 365 days a year.

• ◆ • ◆ •

Father, I want to be known as one who celebrates Your
coming every day of the year. It's great to focus on the
Christ Child at Christmas, but please remind me daily
what an amazing gift Your Son's coming was! Amen.

The Christmas Story

• ◆ • ◆ •

*These commandments that I give you today are to be on
your hearts. Impress them on children. Talk about them
when you sit at home and when you walk along the road,
when you lie down and when you get up.*
Deut. 6:6–7 niv

Sometimes we get so busy that we forget to share the
Christmas story with our children and grandchildren.
We're more interested in prepping Christmas dinner,
wrapping the gifts, and making sure everyone gets along.
We don't remember to pause and read the story from
Luke. Oh, but we should! That story is the foundation of
our gathering, after all. You can make it interactive, too!
Ask the kids (and even the adults) to play the role of the
shepherds, wise men, Mary, Joseph, etc. What fun you'll
have, sharing the story and making memories together.

• ◆ • ◆ •

*I needed the reminder, Lord! The Christmas story needs to
be the pivotal moment in our celebration. Please don't ever
let me forget that Christmas Day is all about You! Amen.*

God-Pleasers

• ◆ • ◆ •

For am I now seeking the approval of man, or of God?
Or am I trying to please man? If I were still trying to
please man, I would not be a servant of Christ.
GALATIANS 1:10 ESV

It's not always easy to remember that our work is for God, not people. From the time we're young we set out to please others—teachers, parents, friends, and so on. Then as we get older, we continue on in our people-pleasing ways, seeking to make professors, bosses, future in-laws, and many others happy. Even in our golden years we find ourselves wanting to please our grown children. There's never a point when we're free from the temptation to make others happy. Only when we let go of the desire to please people and set our sights on pleasing God alone, will we feel true release and joy. Our work has to be for Him and Him alone.

• ◆ • ◆ •

Father, may we, as a family, seek to please You above all others.
From the youngest to the oldest in our circle, may we lay down our
desire to be people pleasers and choose only to be God-pleasers. Amen.

Starlight, Star Bright

* ◆ * ◆ *

God made two great lights—the greater light to govern the day
and the lesser light to govern the night. He also made the stars.
GENESIS 1:16 NIV

There's nothing better than a starry night to bring out the dreamer in us. We gaze up at those twinkling lights, God's radiant nighttime diamonds, and sigh—in part because of their beauty, and in part because we are so in awe of the One who placed them there. That same amazing, dazzling light appeared two thousand years ago as shepherds watched their flocks, and again as wise men made the trek to find the Christ Child. The nighttime skies have always led others to the Lord. So, set your eyes on things above, and worship the One who sets the stars on display in the nighttime sky!

* ◆ * ◆ *

Father, it's the same sky! The same stars! They've been there all along,
bringing wonder and awe, and pointing to You, pointing to Your
Son. May a starlit sky always remind us of Your love for us. Amen.

Christmas Service

• ◆ • ◆ •

*Gather all the people—the elders, the children,
and even the babies. Call the bridegroom from
his quarters and the bride from her private room.*
JOEL 2:16 NLT

Many follow the age-old tradition of meeting together for Christmas Eve (or Christmas Day) service at their local church. There's truly no sweeter time of year to gather together. Everything is so festive and holy. And the idea of coming together in corporate worship as we celebrate is so fitting. After all, the Christian church got its foundation (Jesus) at Christmas. If that baby hadn't come, we probably wouldn't even meet in churches every Sunday to study and learn more about our faith, would we? So link arms! Gather together. Worship as you've never worshipped before. He is worthy!

• ◆ • ◆ •

*Lord, thank You for the freedom to gather with fellow believers,
not just at Christmastime but year-round. You are worthy
of our praise. May our hearts be united as we celebrate
what You've done for us. Amen.*

A Life-Changing Babe

• ◆ • ◆ •

Children are a gift from the LORD;
they are a reward from him.
PSALM 127:3 NLT

Those who are parents (or grandparents, aunts, uncles, godparents, etc.) know the joy a new baby can bring. And with that baby comes change: big change! Schedule changes, dietary changes, financial changes, priority changes, changes in social interactions. . .whew! Having a child changes pretty much everything! It was the same when the Christ Child came. His arrival changed everything, not just for Mary and Joseph, but the shepherds, the wise men, and ultimately us, His people! If that precious child had not arrived, life would have gone on as usual. Oh, but when a baby arrives (especially the King of kings) everything gets rattled (pun intended).

• ◆ • ◆ •

Thank You for rattling our lives by sending Your
Son, Lord! Talk about a life-changing baby!
I'm so grateful for His arrival! Amen.

The Greatest Gift

• ◆ • ◆ •

And now these three remain: faith, hope and love.
But the greatest of these is love.
1 CORINTHIANS 13:13 NIV

So many wonderful gifts under the tree! Delightful, well-thought-out gifts, wrapped with lovely ribbons and bows. Still, there's a greater gift and it's one that doesn't cost a penny: love. When those not-so-easy-to-love folks show up on Christmas Day, give the greatest gift. When they threaten to undo all of your hard work with their negative attitudes, consider your love to them as a "ribbons and bows" offering. It won't be easy. Loving the unlovable rarely is. But that's exactly what God did for us when He sent His Son, after all!

• ◆ • ◆ •

Lord, I'm so grateful for Your love. You've loved me through some tough seasons when I didn't make it easy. Now show me how to do the same to others, so this Christmas season can be love-filled! Amen.

All Snug in Their Beds

· ◆ · ◆ ·

In peace I will both lie down and sleep;
for you alone, O Lord, make me dwell in safety.
PSALM 4:8 ESV

How many times we've quoted the familiar poem about the children being snug in their beds on the night before Christmas. Unfortunately, it doesn't always work out that way! Getting the kids settled down on Christmas Eve can be tough, and the night gets even tougher as dad works to put together bikes and trikes and as mom scurries around doing last-minute preparations for incoming Christmas Day guests. Whew! Talk about exhausting! Still, there's such a whimsical feeling when you peek in the bedroom door at those (finally!) sleeping children. You can only imagine what they're dreaming as they await Christmas morning!

· ◆ · ◆ ·

What precious memories, Lord! Christmas Eve. Christmas morning.
I love all of it! Sure, it's chaotic at times but You're right there,
at the center of it all. Thank You for this precious season, Father! Amen.

Giving Away Your Toys

• ◆ • ◆ •

*"Do not lay up for yourselves treasures on earth, where moth
and rust destroy and where thieves break in and steal,
but lay up for yourselves treasures in heaven, where neither
moth nor rust destroys and where thieves do not break in and
steal. For where your treasure is, there your heart will be also."*
MATTHEW 6:19–21 ESV

Here's a fun idea at Christmastime, one guaranteed
to get everyone in the right frame of mind. Before
buying gifts for the kids, why not suggest that they
each give away one gift from a previous Christmas (to a
homeless shelter or other). If you don't have children in
your home, consider giving away some of your own toys
to make room for the new. Go through your clothes, your
knickknacks, etc. and purge, purge, purge! You'll feel so
good when you're able to bless others with your stuff and
you'll be making room for those incoming gifts, all at the
same time.

• ◆ • ◆ •

*Lord, I have so much stuff already. It doesn't make any sense to
hoard things when I could be blessing others. Help me choose wisely,
Father. I want to give to those who are in need. Amen.*

Emotional Highs and Lows

• ◆ • ◆ •

Therefore, my beloved brothers, be steadfast, immovable,
always abounding in the work of the Lord, knowing
that in the Lord your labor is not in vain.
1 Corinthians 15:58 esv

There's nothing like the holiday season to draw emotions to the surface, both good and bad. We're elated by the idea of gifts and food, but overwhelmed by the idea that we have to purchase those gifts and make that food. Many times we're dealing with losses or pain during the holidays, which only serves to exaggerate already volatile emotions. What is God's heart for us during the Christmas season? How would He choose for us to deal with our emotions during this time of year? His greatest longing is that we keep our eyes on Jesus, His Son. He wants us to experience both the peace and the joy of the Christ Child, no matter what we're going through. It seems impossible at times, but it's not.

• ◆ • ◆ •

Lord, thank You for leveling out my emotions.
I need that, Father! Keep me walking close to You,
controlled by Your spirit, not the ups and downs of life. Amen.

From Heaven to Earth

• ◆ ◆ •

*"'He will wipe every tear from their eyes. There will be
no more death' or mourning or crying or pain,
for the old order of things has passed away."*
REVELATION 21:4 NIV

How we ponder the magnificence of heaven! We let our imaginations run wild as we picture streets of gold, gates of pearl, and mansions for all. We can't fathom how glorious it will be to spend eternity in God's presence. Surely we will never ever want to leave, once we've experienced it. Thinking of it this way puts Jesus's gift into perspective. He left heaven—blissful, perfect heaven—to come to earth, where He had to deal with pain, agony, weather issues, financial struggles, relationship issues, and more. Can you imagine leaving perfection for imperfection? The leap from heaven to earth was a huge one, but He did it just for us.

• ◆ ◆ •

*I can't fathom leaving heaven, Lord! I really can't. What a gift Your
Son gave by coming from such splendor to the daily grind on earth.
How can I ever thank You enough? I praise You, Lord. Amen.*

Heart Matters

• ◆ • ◆ •

My flesh and my heart may fail, but God is the strength of my heart and my portion forever.
PSALM 73:26 ESV

God wants us to guard our hearts all year-round, but they seem to be particularly vulnerable during the holidays. Empty nesters struggle when their grown children won't be coming home for the holidays. The "planners" get offended when others want to take over and change the plan. Those who feel left out curl up into a ball and go into "woe is me" state. The whole thing can be very overwhelming! But God. . .Yes, God wants to stir our hearts to action: to extend grace, to forgive, and to move the focus from ourselves to others. This truly can be the best Christmas ever, but it starts with a heart shift. There's no better day than today!

• ◆ • ◆ •

Lord, I confess I sometimes deal with heart issues during the holidays. My emotions are like a pendulum, swinging back and forth. This year, please guard my heart. I give it to You, knowing I can trust You fully. Amen.

Faithfulness

• ◆ • ◆ •

It is of the Lord's mercies that we are not consumed,
because his compassions fail not. They are new
every morning: great is thy faithfulness.
LAMENTATIONS 3:22–23 KJV

If you ever begin to question God's faithfulness, just reflect on His Christmas gift. . .Jesus. Why would a Father part with a Son, even for thirty-three and a half years—if not out of love? And if propelled by love, (which we know to be true), then surely we can begin to fathom God's faithfulness to us. What does He ask in response? Faithfulness! He wants us to be as dedicated to Him as is humanly possible, to give our hearts, our acts of service, our lives to Him. Yes, He gave the best Christmas gift of all, but God is waiting to see if we will give our greatest gift in response. . .our faithfulness.

• ◆ • ◆ •

Lord, You're so faithful. How You've proven that, time and
time again. I have no doubt in my mind that You adore me.
I give myself to You afresh this season, and remain dedicated
and faithful to follow You all the days of my life. Amen.

Pets

• ◆ • ◆ •

The godly care for their animals,
but the wicked are always cruel.
PROVERBS 12:10 NLT

Pet lovers have so much fun at Christmastime. Of course they love spoiling Fido year-round, but Christmas gives an additional excuse for loading up the pet stocking with bones, toys, sweaters, and treats. In fact, many folks enjoy shopping for the family pet as much as they do for the kids! Owning and caring for a pet is a big responsibility and not everyone is up for it. If you're not able to have a pet of your own, perhaps you could donate to a local animal shelter during the holiday season or provide goodies for a neighbor's pet. There's nothing more satisfying than watching a pup's tail wag in glee. That's the sweetest "Thank you!" there is.

• ◆ • ◆ •

Lord, this year I'm reminded of all of those sweet pups
in shelters who need a home. I pray that you would give
them all they need—arms to wrap around them and sweet
words to be spoken over them by loving owners. Amen.

Merging Families

• ◆ • ◆ •

But the fruit of the Spirit is love, joy, peace, forbearance,
kindness, goodness, faithfulness, gentleness and self-control.
Against such things there is no law.
GALATIANS 5:22–23 NIV

Great-aunt Susie. Cousin Joe. Grandma Milly. Fourteen grandchildren and great-grandchildren. Perhaps there's no greater time than Christmas to see the merging of ages, personalities, and habits. Fitting all of those people—and their gifts—into one home can be a challenge! But that's what the holidays are all about! God loves it when His kids merge lives (and forces) to share the season of the Savior's birth. So don't fret over your differences. Celebrate them. . .and while you're at it, celebrate the reason for the season.

• ◆ • ◆ •

I love my family, Lord. Sure, we're different from each other.
Some are quirkier than others. And when we get together it's
not always easy. . .but it's so worth it. Thank You so much
for bringing us together, Father. Amen.

The Little Extras

• ◆ • ◆ •

*Now to him who is able to do immeasurably more than all
we ask or imagine, according to his power that is at work
within us, to him be glory in the church and in Christ Jesus
throughout all generations, for ever and ever! Amen.*
EPHESIANS 3:20–21 NIV

Don't you just love those people who go the extra
mile? The woman who thinks to add ribbons and
bows to every package. The man who goes out of his
way to pick out the perfect gift for his wife, tailored to
her particular likes. Yes, it's the little things that mean
so much. When someone goes above and beyond, we're
blessed beyond belief because it's a sign they've been
paying attention to our likes and dislikes. May we be just
as attentive to others, so that we can go the extra mile
this holiday season.

• ◆ • ◆ •

*Lord, I'm so grateful for those "above and beyond" people You've
placed in my life. They're such a blessing. May I glean from them
so that I, too, can become as attentive and caring. Amen.*

Drawing Close to the Savior

• ◆ • ◆ •

Then the man said, "Lord, I believe,"
and he worshiped him.
JOHN 9:38 NIV

So many things threaten to pull us away from Jesus during the holiday season. Stress. Money woes. Family sagas. Shopping. More shopping. Cooking. Christmas programs at church and school. More shopping. Planning. Wrapping. More shopping. Unwrapping. Eating. We can get so caught up in the "stuff" that we forget to spend daily time in our Savior's presence. That's when it's important to remember the stable. . .the baby, the gift from heaven. When we pause to remind ourselves that He came as our gift, we can't help but want to draw close. That's His heart's desire, and should be ours, too.

• ◆ • ◆ •

Lord, I want to draw close to You this Christmas season,
closer than ever before. Help me look beyond the crazy
schedule to that sweet, intimate time with You. Amen.

Gathered Together

* ◆ * ◆ *

*"For where two or three gather together as
my followers, I am there among them."*
MATTHEW 18:20 NLT

There's something so special about gathering
together with people we love, especially when there's
yummy food involved. If you think about it, the idea of
table fellowship started the night of the last supper, when
Jesus spent His final meal with His disciples. And that
same love, that same sweet spirit, can be with us, even
now, as we gather around the table with loved ones on
Christmas Day. In fact, we can celebrate togetherness
all year-round. There's strength in numbers. The Bible
confirms this with the verse above. God is always right
there in the midst of us when we gather in His Name. So
let's spend this holiday season doing just that.

* ◆ * ◆ *

*Lord, I love table fellowship. There's something so sweet
about gathering around the table with those I love,
especially as we celebrate the birth of Your Son.
Thank You for this amazing privilege. Amen.*

Commercial Christmas

• ◆ • ◆ •

So then, just as you received Christ Jesus as Lord, continue to live
your lives in him, rooted and built up in him, strengthened in the
faith as you were taught, and overflowing with thankfulness.
COLOSSIANS 2:6–7 NIV

So many people fret over how commercial Christmas
has become (and it has) but what if you took a
different approach this year? Instead of complaining,
or making a big deal about secular Christmas songs in
stores, why not greet everyone with a resounding, "Merry
Christmas" and use the opportunity to share the love of
Christ wherever you go? Just think about it this way: At
no other time of year is it possible to express your faith
so freely. So, when you're standing in line, paying for
that Christmas toy for the child in your life, reach out
to the young mom behind you. Take advantage of the
opportunity to spread the real reason for the season.

• ◆ • ◆ •

Lord, may I learn how to see beyond the commercialism
of Christmas to the real reason, but in doing so,
may I exhibit love to all I meet. Amen.

Christmas Music

• ◆ • ◆ •

He put a new song in my mouth, a hymn of praise to our God.
Many will see and fear the LORD and put their trust in him.
PSALM 40:3 NIV

If you're a music lover, then Christmas is the season for you! It seems, no matter where you go, carols rings out. Many are silly and share tales of Santa and reindeer. Others are tender and sweet, reflecting back on that holy night when the Christ Child entered the world. Oh, isn't it wonderful to hear songs of the season ring out? And nothing unifies us at Christmastime like caroling or sharing in a candlelight service as "Silent Night" is sung in one corporate voice. Music is one way of praising, so feel free to share the joy in song, not just at Christmastime, but all year long.

• ◆ • ◆ •

My heart is filled with song today, Lord! I can't help but
sing out my praises to You during this special season.
What a blessed privilege, to praise You in song. Amen.

Christmas Morning

* ◆ • ◆ •

Let me hear of your unfailing love each morning, for I am
trusting you. Show me where to walk, for I give myself to you.
PSALM 143:8 NLT

Many people don't care for mornings. They hit the
snooze button on the alarm clock and roll over
for another ten minutes of sleep. Oh, but heaven help
the person who oversleeps on Christmas morning. (Can
you imagine the children, all piling onto mom and dad's
bed? Chaos!) So out of bed we spring. We bound toward
the living room to find the children gathered around the
tree, their eyes on the prize(s). But traditions are in order
here! French toast for breakfast (or the traditional fare
of your choice). The reading of the Christmas story. A
sweet time of prayer, and then. . .dive in! It's every man,
woman, and child for himself!

• ◆ • ◆ •

Lord, how I love Christmas morning. No matter the ages
of those I spend the day with, it's fun to wake up on the
twenty-fifth of December with excitement in my heart.
May I never lose my childlike wonder, I pray. Amen.

Holly Jolly

• ◆ • ◆ •

Though you have not seen him, you love him; and even
though you do not see him now, you believe in him and are
filled with an inexpressible and glorious joy, for you are
receiving the goal of your faith, the salvation of your souls.
1 PETER 1:8–9 NIV

*W*hat does it mean to have a holly jolly Christmas?
To be jolly means you forget about all of the
stresses and just let loose and have a blast. You're not
thinking about the bills or the messy house. You're
not even worried about what people will think about
that chocolate pie you tried to bake. No, a "holly jolly"
Christmas is one that casts insecurities and troubles aside
and focuses on the joy of the season, not the pain. It's
one that chooses to share the good and not the bad, a
message of hope, no matter the pain. You can choose to
have a holly jolly Christmas this season, no matter what's
going on around you. Then watch as your good cheer
spreads to all you meet.

• ◆ • ◆ •

Lord, I'm asking for a rejuvenation in my heart. I don't want to
fake it, Lord. May the "holly jolly" spirit truly capture my heart,
my mind, my imagination. What a blessing this will be! Amen.

State of Mind

• ◆ • ◆ •

*Those who live according to the flesh have their minds set
on what the flesh desires; but those who live in accordance
with the Spirit have their minds set on what the Spirit
desires. The mind governed by the flesh is death,
but the mind governed by the Spirit is life and peace.*
ROMANS 8:5–6 NIV

It's so hard to rise above the flesh, especially during the holidays. People grate on us and we want to get bitter or frustrated. They overlook us and we want to get our feelings hurt. They run us over with their plans, their strategies, and we want to kick back by demanding or own way. All of these situations have one thing in common: We "want to" do something. We get to choose how we react, and our choice always comes back to our state of mind. If we have our minds set on things above, if we're really focused on what's best for everyone (and ultimately for the Lord), we'll guard our reactions more carefully. May our thoughts be His thoughts and our reactions His reactions.

• ◆ • ◆ •

*Lord, I'm setting my mind on things above.
I want Your will, Your plan. Guard me as I
seek to react as You would react, Father! Amen.*

Persistence

• ◆ • ◆ •

And let us not grow weary of doing good,
for in due season we will reap, if we do not give up.
GALATIANS 6:9 ESV

Oh, how much we have to learn about persistence. We give up so easily. Perhaps the greatest example we have of persistence is that of a loving God, giving the Israelites opportunity after opportunity. He consistently gave them chances to follow Him, no matter how many times they got it wrong. Ultimately, God persisted in the most remarkable way of all—by sending His Son to redeem those who couldn't seem to do it on their own. Can you imagine how different things would be if God had just given up on the Israelites? What if He'd said, "Forget it. They're never going to get their act together." Oh, but He never gave up! Instead, He sent them the best gift ever: the Messiah!

• ◆ • ◆ •

Thank You for not giving up on us, Lord.
You're so persistent. May I learn from Your example, Father,
and never give up on Your promises. Amen.

A Change in Perspective

• ◆ • ◆ •

Whatever you do, work heartily,
as for the Lord and not for men.
COLOSSIANS 3:23 ESV

It totally changes our perspective when we do our work "as unto the Lord." When we're prepping for the office Christmas party, when we're sending out Christmas cards, when we're dealing with that never-ending shopping list for the grandkids. . .we can do it all for Him. Keeping our focus on the Lord helps a lot because our "Why in the world do I have to do this?" problem disappears. It morphs into, "Wow, I get to do this!" which is a completely different mindset. So work for Him and watch how your heart changes this Christmas season.

• ◆ • ◆ •

Lord, it's all for You. Truly. May every bit of work
I'm doing come under the "all for Jesus" umbrella. Amen.

'Twas the Night Before Christmas

· ◆ · ◆ ·

Then God put him in the place of honor at his right
hand as Prince and Savior. He did this so the people
of Israel would repent of their sins and be forgiven.
ACT 5:31 NLT

Oh, how we love to quote the poem, " 'Twas the Night
Before Christmas." The joy of that story is conta-
gious, after all. But there's a real "night before Christmas"
story that's even more exciting than the Santa Claus
version. It involves a young couple, an inn, and a stable.
Their "night before Christmas" (or "hours before
delivery") tale was fraught with adventure, curiosity,
inspiration, and wonder. Best of all, it was written by the
world's greatest Author of all time, the Lord Himself.
Now that's a tale worth sharing!

· ◆ · ◆ ·

Lord, may I never forget what transpired in the hours
before Your Son's birth. What a remarkable story,
one that I must pass to future generations! Amen.

Candy Cane Promises

We always carry around in our body the death of Jesus,
so that the life of Jesus may also be revealed in our body.
2 CORINTHIANS 4:10 NIV

ost everyone knows the legend of the candy cane, of the candy maker who started with white candy, to symbolize the Virgin birth and the purity of the Savior. Then he wove in red candy, to represent the blood of Jesus, who gave His life on Calvary. Finally, he shaped the candy into the letter J so that we would never forget Jesus, the reason for the season. God's promises to us are real, all year-round! Whether that little story is true or not, we can still remember all of those things when we look at candy canes. And to top it all off, they're tasty, too!

• ◆ • ◆ •

What a lovely symbol of Your love for us, Lord! Purity, shed blood,
and a Savior, who gave His very life for me. What a lovely example
the candy cane is. Thank You for this reminder. Amen.

Mary, Did You Know?

· ◆ · ◆ ·

He replied, "Blessed rather are those
who hear the word of God and obey it."
LUKE 11:28 NIV

There's a popular song, sung at Christmastime, titled "Mary, Did You Know?" It raises so many fascinating questions about the virgin mother. Did she know, while carrying the baby safely inside of her that He would one day minister and heal and ultimately give His life for mankind? Surely she could not have fathomed what birthing the Son of God would mean—for her life and the lives of all mankind. Did she lie awake at night, wondering what the future held for that precious babe, or did she (as scripture suggests) tuck all these things away in her heart and place her trust in the God of the universe? We may never know what Mary went through, but we're so grateful for her willingness to do all that God asked her to do.

· ◆ · ◆ ·

Lord, I want to follow through, as Mary did,
even if I don't know how things are going to turn out.
Give me faith to obey, even when it's tough, Father. Amen.

The Wonder of it All

• ◆ • ◆ •

You are the God of great wonders!
You demonstrate your awesome power among the nations.
PSALM 77:14 NLT

Have you ever thought about the word *wonder*? A "wonder" is a marvelous act, far above anything we could imagine. Only God can perform wonders. He takes our breath away. A virgin birth? No problem! He's got this. An angelic choir? He's got that, too. A miraculous visit from magi? Of course! There's nothing our great God can't do. He's a wonder-working God—parting seas, healing the sick, and offering new life to those who feel they have nothing left to live for. What an amazing, holy God we serve!

• ◆ • ◆ •

Lord, I worship You! I'm in awe of all You do.
Wonder of wonders! You alone are capable of
miracles, Father. How I praise You. Amen.

Advent

• ◆ • ◆ •

"All right then, the Lord himself will give you the sign. Look!
The virgin will conceive a child! She will give birth to a son
and will call him Immanuel (which means 'God is with us')."
ISAIAH 7:14 NLT

The anticipation of Christmas gifts arriving is half the fun, isn't it! We prep everything from the house to the food to the linens, all for our guests. We "make ready" our hearts and homes. Counting down the days during the Advent season is an amazing tradition to pass on to our children. The entire process helps us focus our hearts and prepare, prepare, prepare for the big day, when we celebrate the Christ Child. Talk about fanfare! Talk about ushering in the season! Advent is the arrival of someone very special, and there's truly no one more special than the King of kings and Lord of lords!

• ◆ • ◆ •

Lord, I anticipate the celebration of Your birth and I anticipate
Your return. May I forever be in an "advent" frame of mind,
excited about spending time with You. Amen.

Highly Favored

• ◆ • ◆ •

For it is You who blesses the righteous man, O Lord,
You surround him with favor as with a shield.
PSALM 5:12 NASB

It's amazing to think that God would surround us with favor as a shield. Usually we think of a shield as a form of protection. But really, favor is a form of protection, too. When God "favors" us, our enemies don't stand a chance. That's how it was when the magi received God's favor. Herod didn't stand a chance. That's how it was when Mary received God's favor. The villagers who could've destroyed her with their gossip didn't stand a chance. God is in the business of protecting His kids, so prepare yourself for His favor this Christmas. Plan to wear it as a shield!

• ◆ • ◆ •

Lord, thank You for Your protection! So many times
You've intervened, showing me favor when I didn't
deserve it. I'm so grateful, Father. Amen.

Making a List and Checking it Twice

• ◆ • ◆ •

*Trust in the LORD with all your heart and lean
not on your own understanding; in all your ways
submit to him, and he will make your paths straight.*
PROVERBS 3:5–6 NIV

Perhaps you're a list maker. You're the organized
type. You put together lists for meals, for Christmas
shopping, even for the kinds of cookies you plan to bake.
You can't function without your list. Being organized is
critical, especially during the holidays. But sometimes
tossing your list and going with the flow is just as much
fun. So what if a snowstorm messes up your plans to see
Christmas lights? Make some hot cocoa and cookies and
go with the flow. Play board games or watch a Christmas
movie. So what if the store is sold out of the one big
present you'd hoped to buy little Susie? Order it online
or wait until after the Christmas rush to get it. The point
is, you can relax. . .even if everything on the list doesn't
get done.

• ◆ • ◆ •

*Lord, I want to relax, to toss my list, and go with the flow.
But I'm going to need Your help, for sure! I prefer things to
go my way. I guess that's what trust is all about, Father,
so I choose to trust You this season. Amen.*

All I Want for Christmas

• ◆ • ◆ •

When I was a child, I spoke as a child, I understood as a child,
I thought as a child; but when I became a man, I put away childish
things. For now we see in a mirror, dimly, but then face to face.
Now I know in part, but then I shall know just as I also am known.
1 CORINTHIANS 13:11–12 NKJV

If someone asked the question: "What would you like for Christmas if you could only have one thing?" how would you answer? What if they added the words: "Money is no object!" That would certainly open the conversation to new possibilities, wouldn't it! Maybe you'd ask for a trip to an exotic location or for an expensive home or vehicle. No matter what your "dream gift" might be, remember. . .you were already given the gift of all gifts through the Savior, Jesus Christ. He was, and is, a gift that keeps on giving!

• ◆ • ◆ •

Lord, I'm such a dreamer! I love the idea of traveling and
of owning beautiful things. Thank You for the reminder that
I already have the most beautiful gift of all! Jesus has taken
up residence in my heart and has given me eternal life.
What a precious gift! I'm so grateful, Father. Amen.

Christmas Luggage

• ◆ • ◆ •

*Therefore, since we are surrounded by such a great cloud of witnesses,
let us throw off everything that hinders and the sin that so easily
entangles. And let us run with perseverance the race marked out for us.*
HEBREWS 12:1 NIV

Oh, the luggage we haul when we're traveling! In
spite of restrictions from airlines, we still load up,
carrying as much as we can. We don't want to get to our
destination without the necessary clothing items, after
all! There's only one problem with luggage: It weighs
us down! Sometimes we get to the airport and discover
our bag is over the weight limit! The same is true with
emotional baggage. Sometimes we refuse to ditch it
and it ends up working against us, especially during the
holidays. So, if you're hauling around any unnecessary
baggage this season, let it go! Dump it before it starts to
weigh you down!

• ◆ • ◆ •

*Lord, I'll admit, sometimes I overpack. I hang on to things
I shouldn't. When it comes to my emotional health, though,
I want to let go of the things that have become burdensome.
Please help me toss those things to the curb, Father! Amen.*

Cheer

• ◆ • ◆ •

These things I have spoken unto you, that in me ye might
have peace. In the world ye shall have tribulation:
but be of good cheer; I have overcome the world.
JOHN 16:33 KJV

The words "be of good cheer" are familiar from this
popular verse, but where does "cheer" come from?
Can we manufacture it by partying with the right people
or singing carols at the top of our lungs? Can we "be
cheerful" without intervention? True Christmas cheer
comes from an abiding relationship with the Lord. He
infuses us with joy—not just the kind you hear about in
Christmas songs, but life-changing joy. Once we're joy-
filled, the "good cheer" is a natural by-product. We can't
help but smile at folks in the grocery store or wave at the
neighbor as he walks by. Joy is our energizer!

• ◆ • ◆ •

I rely on Your joy, Father, and not just during the holidays! I need to
"be of good cheer" year-round, which is why I depend on Your daily
infusions! Thank You for the reminder that I don't have to work at
being cheerful. It's a gift, and one I won't take for granted. Amen.

Do You Hear What I Hear?

"My ears had heard of you but
now my eyes have seen you."
JOB 42:5 NIV

It's so fascinating to think about what sounds rang out on the night of the Christ Child's birth. The lowing of cattle. The groans of a mother in labor. The sound of voices from passersby outside the stable. The joyous songs of angels in the heavenly realm. The chatter of anxious shepherds. The bleating of sheep as their caretakers headed off toward Bethlehem. The whistling of the wind overhead. The still, small voice of the Holy Spirit, speaking words of comfort. And finally. . .through it all. . .the piercing cry of a newborn, gasping for air for the very first time. Oh, what heavenly sounds. And if our ear is tuned in, we can still hear the still, small voice whispering, "Come. Come to the stable and watch as your lives are changed!"

What a holy night it must have been, Father. . .the night
Your Son was born. Oh, how I wish I could have heard
those sounds. Even now, I'm listening for Your voice, Lord.
Speak, I'm listening. Amen.

God's Heart for His Children

• ◆ • ◆ •

So we have come to know and to believe the love
that God has for us. God is love, and whoever abides
in love abides in God, and God abides in him.
1 JOHN 4:16 ESV

Do you know what it's like to win someone's heart? As young brides we celebrate the fact that we've won the heart of our mate. As we give birth to our children, we take joy in the fact that they've won our hearts (and vice versa) from day one. Truly, when you have someone's heart, you would be willing to lay down your life for that person, to come to their rescue, should they need you. That's exactly what God did for us in Bethlehem, that amazing night. We'd snagged a piece of His heart and He wanted to take care of us. In turn, we now have Him in our hearts. It's a love-love relationship, and it all started in a stable, with a precious baby boy, one who surely captured His mama's heart, right off the bat.

• ◆ • ◆ •

Lord, You've won my heart and I've won Yours!
Thank You for loving me so much that You sent Your Son.
I feel supremely loved, Father. Amen.

Abounding. . .and Rebounding

• ◆ • ◆ •

I press on toward the goal to win the prize for which
God has called me heavenward in Christ Jesus.
PHILIPPIANS 3:14 NIV

Not every Christmas season goes as planned. In fact, many of them fall flat, despite our best efforts. We do our best to remember the reason for the season, but even that gets tough when we're struggling with emotional or financial woes. The truth is, no matter what you've faced in the past, you can still rebound and come back stronger than ever. Maybe last Christmas was a bust. This one doesn't have to be. Maybe last year you overspent. This year can be different. Point is, we can rebound and celebrate the spiritual abundance that this holiday season brings.

• ◆ • ◆ •

Lord, I'm glad You're a God who helps people rebound! I've messed
up a lot of things in my life but You're always there to give second
chances. Thanks for making this Christmas the best ever. Amen.

To Everything a Season

• • ◆ •

There is a time for everything,
and a season for every activity under the heavens.
ECCLESIASTES 3:1 NIV

*C*an you imagine if baby Jesus had been born in the twenty-first century? How different things would have been. Picture the shepherds, barreling into Bethlehem in their trucks. And what about the wise men? They would've been looking in their rearview mirror to make sure Herod wasn't on their tail as they booked it out of Bethlehem. And Mary? Would she have chosen to keep the baby? It's a legitimate question, isn't it? Factor in the innkeeper, Joseph, and all of the other players, and try to picture their responses in the twenty-first century. Hard to imagine, for sure! No, God knew just what He was doing, sending His Son exactly when He did. There is truly an appointed season for everything under the sun. . .including the coming of the Son.

• ◆ • ◆ •

I love how You time things, Lord. It doesn't always make much
sense in the moment, but in the grand scheme of things it makes
perfect sense. Thank You for sending Your Son at just the right
moment. What a marvelous God You are! Amen.

Blessed to Bless

• ◆ • ◆ •

"I will make you into a great nation, and I will bless you;
I will make your name great, and you will be a blessing."
GENESIS 12:2 NIV

Perhaps you've heard the expression, "I'm blessed
to be a blessing." Some would equate this with
prosperity teaching, but the words are true, no matter
your economic level. Whenever God pours out His
blessing on you (financially, emotionally, relationally, or
otherwise), He's doing it so that you have an abundance
to share with others. Hoarding it would serve no
purpose, after all. So, as you consider your abundance this
Christmas season, remember: God loves a cheerful giver.
You have truly been blessed so that you can pour it out
on others. So let the blessings flow!

• ◆ • ◆ •

Lord, I want to pour myself out for others. You've blessed me
with mercy, grace, forgiveness. You've made sure I have all I need
financially. Now help me pass on the blessings, Father! Amen.

The Most Wonderful Time of the Year

· ◆ · ◆ ·

*Therefore my heart is glad, and my whole
being rejoices; my flesh also dwells secure.*
PSALM 16:9 ESV

For many, the Christmas season really is the most wonderful time of the year. It's filled with childlike wonder, cookies from grandma, and ham with all the trimmings from mom. It's dad, sneaking down the stairs on Christmas morning to put together that last bike, and grandpa, snoozing in his recliner after all of the gifts have been opened. It's Great-aunt Margaret, heading back into the kitchen for her second piece of chocolate pie. It's the Sunday school group, gathering together to sing carols at a nursing home. Best of all, it's the spirit of joy that permeates everyone you come in contact with during the holiday season. When the Christ Child is at the center of the celebration, there's much reason for joy, after all!

· ◆ · ◆ ·

*Thank You for this season, Father. It truly is the
most wonderful time of the year. My heart
is filled with joy and gratitude. Amen.*

Covenant

• ◆ • ◆ •

He remembers his covenant forever,
the promise he made, for a thousand generations.
PSALM 105:8 NIV

God has always had a special place in His heart for the Jewish people. His covenant with them goes all the way back to Abraham, who was promised that he would be the father of many nations. The birth of Abraham's son Isaac set in motion a chain of events that would change the world and new lineage that would one day include Jesus Christ. What an amazing thought! And God's covenant expanded to include us—those outside the Jewish faith—when Jesus was born. He came from the covenanted lineage, and yet opened His arms wide, even to those outside the family. What a loving God we serve!

• ◆ • ◆ •

Thank You for including me, Father! I wasn't part
of the family tree, but You grafted me in. I'm forever
grateful to be part of the family, Lord. Amen.

Wrapped up with Ribbons and Bows

• ◆ • ◆ •

Each one must give as he has decided in his heart, not reluctantly or under compulsion, for God loves a cheerful giver.
2 CORINTHIANS 9:7 ESV

Oh, how we love to "get." Many of us have closets—and homes—filled with stuff. And we love it when our stuff is presented to us, wrapped up tight with ribbons and bows. What fun to pull all of the decorations off and peek inside the box. Christmas is a great time to receive, of course, but it's so much more fun to give. Prepping gifts for those we love can be the highlight of our day! And when we have a cheerful heart, when we're really thrilled to be able to share gifts with others, it just makes the experience even better. No matter what God calls you to give this Christmas season—gifts, forgiveness, grace, or other—do so with a happy heart and cheerful countenance.

• ◆ • ◆ •

Lord, it's more than just a saying! It truly is more blessed to give than to receive. Thank You so much for teaching me this lesson. Now, show me what You want me to give. I'm ready, Father! Amen.

Jack Frost Nipping at Your Nose

• ◆ • ◆ •

Also, if two lie down together, they will keep warm.
But how can one keep warm alone?
ECCLESIASTES 4:11 NIV

Brr! The Christmas season can be icy! Jack Frost works overtime during the holidays, often snowing us in when we'd rather be shopping or spending time with friends. But there's truly no greater time to gather around the fireplace with the family, to share stories, to roast marshmallows, to talk about life goals, dreams, and plans. Sure, the weather outside might be frightful, but the warmth in your heart can be, well, delightful! So stick together. Stay with those you love. There's power in numbers, sure, but there's also warmth in numbers.

• ◆ • ◆ •

I love those sweet days when we're gathered around the fireplace,
Lord. Being with those I love warms me from the inside out.
I'm so grateful for these precious moments! Thank You, Father! Amen.

A Gentle Answer

• ◆ • ◆ •

A gentle answer turns away wrath,
but a harsh word stirs up anger.
PROVERBS 15:1 NIV

Perhaps there's no greater time of year than Christmas to have a gentle heart. Why? Because the temptation to get hard-hearted is so prevalent during the holidays as folks rush from here to there, frazzled and financially tapped. It's also important to respond kindly because we come in contact with so many people during the Christmas season. Store clerks. Delivery men. Postmen. Co-workers and their spouses. Church members. When we treat all of these people with grace and ease, (especially during tough moments) we diffuse otherwise combustible situations. A gentle answer really can turn things around, so be ready to give one today!

• ◆ • ◆ •

Lord, I don't want to be combustible! I want to have a soft,
gentle answer ready for those who irritate me. Give me the words to
say in the moment, Father! May my words reflect Your heart. Amen.

Ornaments

• ◆ • ◆ •

*Then the servant brought out gold and silver jewelry
and articles of clothing and gave them to Rebekah;
he also gave costly gifts to her brother and to her mother.*
GENESIS 24:53 NIV

Our fascination with ornaments is interesting, isn't it? There's something so touching about those glittery little items. Why do we pile them on our tree? Just for decoration, or is there more? Many times we associate particular ornaments with memories from the past: the darling little rocking horse we bought the year Johnny was born. The adorable snowflake, hand-tatted by grandma the year before she passed away. The faded reindeer, a treasured memento from childhood. Yes, the tree is covered in ornaments, but better than that. . .it tells a story of dozens of lives, people we adore, and many who have passed on. It's a memory tree, an ever-present reminder of the legacy passed on from generations before and generations yet to come.

• ◆ • ◆ •

*I love the memories that flood over me when I look at the
ornaments on my tree, Father. It's bittersweet at times, but I'm
so grateful for such an amazing legacy. Praise You, Lord! Amen.*

Outside of Yourself

• ◆ • ◆ •

If one of you says to them, "Go in peace; keep warm and well fed,"
but does nothing about their physical needs, what good is it?
JAMES 2:16 NIV

We do our best to meet our family's needs during the holidays, and this is great! But if we take the time to really look beyond our own circle, we'll find hundreds—or even thousands—who are struggling. That man on the street corner. That woman in the shelter with her children. That elderly veteran with posttraumatic stress disorder. That lonely neighbor. They all need someone to extend a hand. This year, instead of just focusing on those you can see, spend some time putting together a plan for those you can't. Prepare food, clothing, or other items for those in need. What a blessing you can be!

• ◆ • ◆ •

Father, help me look beyond the wants and wishes of my own family
to the greater need. I want to bless those who are hurting, Lord.
Point me in the right direction, I pray. Amen.

The Heart of Joseph

• ◆ • ◆ •

So he got up, took the child and his mother
during the night and left for Egypt.
MATTHEW 2:14 NIV

Have you ever pondered Joseph's reaction to the news that he would be the human father to the Savior of the world? His actions from start to finish show us several things: First, he loved Mary and didn't want her to be ashamed. Second, his actions reflected his faith when he responded to the angel's words. Third, he cared so much about the baby that he "fathered" with his whole heart, even going so far as to move his family to another country to protect the baby from harm. What an amazing man, and what a role model to us all this Christmas season. May we seek to uplift others, to respond in faith, and to shepherd those who need our love and protection.

• ◆ • ◆ •

Lord, I want to have a heart like Joseph's.
What a wonderful example he is—of Your grace and
goodness. May my heart be as godly as his, I pray. Amen.

The Heart of Mary

• ◆ • ◆ •

*Now the birth of Jesus Christ was on this wise: When
as his mother Mary was espoused to Joseph, before they
came together, she was found with child of the Holy Ghost.*
MATTHEW 1:18 KJV

What would it mean to have the heart of Mary?
Perhaps we could look at it this way: Mary was
pure. Innocent. She faced every emotion: excitement (as
a bride-to-be), fear (after receiving the news from the
angel), anticipation (once the pregnancy was underway),
fear (wondering what others thought of her). Most of
all, she didn't panic. She didn't knee-jerk. She took the
time to think deeply about what the angel had told her
and then took the time to slowly, methodically, trust God
with the outcome. To have the heart of Mary means
we take a deep breath, do our best not to overreact, and
ponder the miracle that's growing inside of us.

• ◆ • ◆ •

*Lord, thank You for giving me such a lovely example!
I don't want to knee-jerk! I want to be pure, innocent,
and trusting, as she was. Work on my heart, I pray. Amen.*

The Heart of Christ

• ◆ • ◆ •

*I pray that out of his glorious riches he may strengthen
you with power through his Spirit in your inner being,
so that Christ may dwell in your hearts through faith.*

EPHESIANS 3:16–17 NIV

We can strive to have a heart like Joseph's, kind and accepting. We can do our best to have the innocence and purity of Mary. But ultimately, we need hearts like Jesus Himself. This is a tougher challenge, because it forces us to forgive when we don't feel like forgiving, to lay down our lives when we'd rather look the other way, and to share His message, even when we're not in the mood to share. To have the heart of Christ means that we always look out for the interests of others, and that we place God's commands above our own wants and wishes. Oh, the payoff is grand! When we have the heart of Christ, we are imbued with power from on high. With Christlike hearts, we witness miracles and live remarkable lives (and not just during the holidays).

• ◆ • ◆ •

*I long to have the heart of Jesus! Please teach me every
single day how to listen for the heartbeat of Christ and
bring my own heartbeat into alignment. Amen.*

Christmas, All Year-Round

• ◆ • ◆ •

*Therefore, my brothers and sisters, you whom
I love and long for, my joy and crown,
stand firm in the Lord in this way, dear friends!*
PHILIPPIANS 4:1 NIV

What a loving God we serve. We honor Him during
every season, and not just because of all of the
blessings He's poured out on us. God is worthy of our
praise every day of the year. Still, we can't help but
celebrate His most sacrificial gift of all: His Son. The
ultimate Christmas present! How can we ever repay such
a gift? We cannot. But we will live our lives to honor
Him, and to say "Thank You, heavenly Father!" with each
action. Indeed, every day of our lives can be Christmas,
if we keep Christ at the center. And each act of worship
will bring honor to Him, just as those wise men did all
those years ago. May we always carry Christmas in our
hearts!

• ◆ • ◆ •

*Lord, I want to have Christmas in my heart, long after
the tree is down and the gifts are put away. May I celebrate
the ultimate gift—Your Son—all year long. Amen.*

We Wish You a Merry Christmas

* ◆ * ◆ *

*We are writing these things so
that you may fully share our joy.*
1 JOHN 1:4 NLT

Remember that lovely Judy Garland song, "Have Yourself a Merry Little Christmas"? Why do you suppose that song gained such popularity? Could it be that listeners loved the idea that they could *choose* to have a merry Christmas? Yes, even during the holidays we get to choose whether or not to have a great attitude and peaceful spirit. This year, and the next and the next, make up your mind to spread Christmas cheer. Make merry wherever you go, keeping alive the true meaning of Christmas, in your heart, your mind, and your actions.

* ◆ * ◆ *

*Merry Christmas, Lord! May it be the resounding theme
of my life. I want to celebrate Your goodness so that others
can see and join in the festivities. I praise You, Father,
no matter the season. Your joy is alive in my heart. Amen.*

About the Author

Janice Thompson, who lives in the Houston area, writes novels, non-fiction, magazine articles, and musical comedies for the stage. The mother of four married daughters, she is quickly adding grandchildren to the family mix.

Also Available from Barbour Books

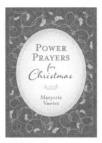

Find them wherever great Christian books are sold!